knitted beanies
&
slouchy hats

0 11557 01378 8

knitted
beanies
&
slouchy
hats

Diane Serviss

STACKPOLE
BOOKS

Dedicated to my husband, Christopher, without whom I would be all drive without direction. Thank you for always being my true north.

Published by
STACKPOLE BOOKS
5067 Ritter Road
Mechanicsburg, PA 17055
www.stackpolebooks.com

Printed in the United States of America

First edition

Cover photograph by Burcu Avsar
Cover design by Caroline Stover

Library of Congress Cataloging-in-Publication Data

Serviss, Diane.
  Knitted beanies & slouchy hats / Diane Serviss.
       pages cm
  Includes index.
  ISBN 978-0-8117-1378-8
1. Knitting—Patterns. 2. Hats. I. Title. II. Title: Knitted beanies and slouchy hats.
  TT825.S46 2014
  746.43'2—dc23
                              2014014862

Contents

Acknowledgments

First and foremost, I need to express much love and appreciation for my husband, Christopher, and our daughters, Caitlin, Samantha, and Natassia. Thank you for your support and patience, for indulging my obsession, and for braving this adventure with me.

I owe a huge debt of gratitude to my friends, family, and mentors, especially those whom I interact with regularly on Facebook. Thank you for your advice and for responding to my endless queries with utter honesty and wisdom. I won't soon forget how you championed me to the finish line.

For your guidance and reassurance, I am much obliged to my wonderful editor, Pam Hoenig. Thank you as well to Stackpole Books; I am grateful for this opportunity.

A very special thanks to photographer Burcu Avsar for bringing my garments to life. I admire your vision and thank you for your efforts.

Introduction

t all began in a little house on a hill in Vermont with a quilted harvest gold sewing chest filled with miraculous things. Cushions stuck with pins, measuring tapes, crochet hooks in every size and color, and a pair of silvery blue aluminum knitting needles that, I will admit, my sister and I used as light sabers in epic *Star Wars* duel reenactments. Below the top tray were vintage knitting magazines that may as well have been written in another language for all the sense they made to me, but the pictures inside were a bounty of inspiration.

There is something magical that occurs when you can take a raw material like yarn and turn it into something tangible, something unique and warm and comforting, something that envelops you and fosters a sense of security. I would marvel at the afghans my Grandmother Simone made, and I would beg my mother to make me caps and clothes for my dolls. The irony was not lost on me that to begin to knit you must cast on, as if to bewitch a needle to do your bidding. These women were sorceresses, as far as I was concerned, but it wasn't until my mid-thirties that I learned this incantation myself.

I have always cherished the heirloom quality of handmade items and the endless possibilities of design that knitting provides. With the help of online videos I taught myself to knit and crochet. With every new lesson and charm I designed a piece to practice these newfound abilities. I have honed my skills as a knitter and designer simultaneously and developed an aesthetic born of necessity and inspired by timelessness.

Soon after I taught myself to knit, my husband expressed a desire to learn as well. He was encouraged by the rhythmic clickety-clack of the needles, the serenity of the process, and the gratification of turning nothing into something. He was spellbound, just as I had been. In 2007 we opened our Pixiebell shop on Etsy (pixiebell.etsy.com) to sell our finished goods, focusing on hats and gloves and scarves, to keep the works in progress and finished objects from overtaking our home and swallowing us whole in some giant wooly vortex.

Since then we have been blessed with great opportunities. My patterns have appeared in magazines, we have worked with stylists for film, television, and print ads, and we have had many celebrity clients. We have grown as artisans and makers and ambassadors of a craft that not only nurtures our creative souls, but also solely provides for our family.

Who could have guessed that an unassuming quilted harvest gold sewing chest could have been the catalyst for such an adventure as this? They say when you write a book it is like taking a journey, and now that I have traveled this road, I tend to agree. In the beginning I did not know that I had so much to say as a designer but I soon realized that I have a voice that needs to be heard in the form of woven bits of yarn and string, a need to cradle and conjure and connect. This book is not only a collection of patterns, but chapters that follow my own pilgrimage from the lightheartedness of childhood to the sophistication of adulthood and all of the stories and spells in between.

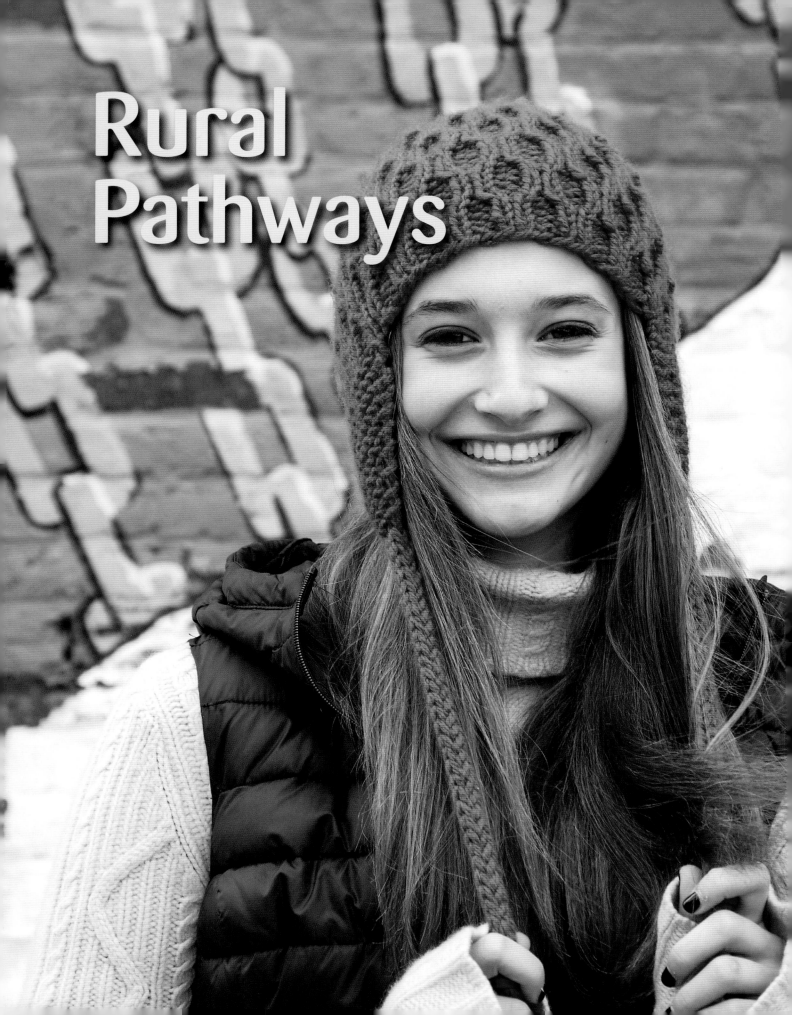

Rural Pathways

The cable pattern of Rural Pathways has a unique rhythm. A tip to help remember if the cable needle needs to go to the front or back, in this pattern, is to note the type of stitch you're putting on the cable needle. Knit stitches will go to the front and purl stitches will go to the back.

FINISHED MEASUREMENTS

Circumference at brim band 19" (48 cm) unstretched, 8" (20 cm) in length from brim edge to crown; will fit head circumference of 20" to 23" (50.5 to 58 cm)

YARN

130 yds (119 m) bulky weight #5 yarn (shown knitted in #730002-0017 Cinnamon, Willow Yarns Burrow, 75% acrylic, 25% wool, 131 yds/120 m per skein)

NEEDLES AND OTHER MATERIALS

- One 16" (40.5 cm) circular knitting needle US 10 (6 mm) or size needed to obtain gauge
- US 10 (6 mm) set of 5 double-pointed needles or size needed to obtain gauge
- Stitch marker
- Cable needle
- Scissors
- Yarn needle

GAUGE

16 sts x 18 rows in cable stitch pattern = 4" (10 cm) square

SPECIAL STITCHES

Left Purl Cross (LPC): Slip 1 st to cable needle, hold cable needle in front of work, purl 1 st from left needle, knit 1 from cable needle.

Right Purl Cross (RPC): Slip 1 st to cable needle, hold cable needle in back of work, knit 1 st from left needle, purl 1 from cable needle.

- Make 2 earflaps, cast on foundation row, and work hat in rounds from bottom edge to crown. Switch from circular needles to double-pointed needles when necessary during crown shaping.
- For photo tutorials on backward loop cast-on, the cable stitches, and making an I-cord, see pages 107, 113–114, and 123–124.

Hat

Using long-tail method and circular needle, CO 24 sts. With RS facing, knit across first ear flap. Using backward loop method, CO 12 sts. With RS facing, knit across second earflap. Place a stitch marker between first and last st and join in the round, being careful not to twist cast-on row.

Rnds 1–4: K1, *p2, k2; rep from * until last 3 sts, p2, k1—72 sts.

Rnd 5: *LPC, RPC; rep from * around.

Rnds 6–9: P1, *k2, p2; rep from * until last 3 sts, k2, p1.

Rnd 10: *RPC, LPC; rep from * around.

Rnds 11–14: K1, *p2, k2; rep from * until last 3 sts, p2, k1.

Rnd 15: *LPC, RPC; rep from * around.

Rnds 16–19: P1, *k2, p2; rep from * until last 3 sts, k2, p1.

Rnd 20: *RPC, LPC; rep from * around.

Rnds 21–24: K1, *p2, k2; rep from * until last 3 sts, p2, k1.

Rnd 25: *LPC, RPC; rep from * around.

Rnds 26–29: P1, *k2, p2; rep from * until last 3 sts, k2, p1.

Rnd 30: *RPC, LPC; rep from * around.

Rnds 31–33: K1, *p2, k2; rep from * until last 3 sts, p2, k1.

Rnd 34: K1, *p2, k2; rep from * until last 3 sts, p2, remove last stitch from needle, transfer stitch marker to right needle, and place last stitch on left needle.

Rnd 35: *K2tog, p2tog; rep from * around—36 sts.

Rnd 36: *K2tog; rep from * around—18 sts.

Rnd 37: *K2tog; rep from * around—9 sts.

Finishing

Cut yarn, leaving an 8" (20.5 cm) tail. Thread yarn needle with end and pick up remaining stitches on knitting needles. Pull tightly to close and secure end. Weave in yarn tails on inside of hat. Secure I-cord tails into center of I-cord. Tie overhand knots in bottoms of both I-cords.

Earflap (make 2)

Using long-tail method and 2 double-pointed needles, CO 4 sts. Knit 40 rows of I-cord. I-cord is made by knitting these 4 stitches. Do not turn your work; the same side should always be facing you. When the row is complete, slide the work to the right end of the dpn. With the working yarn coming around the back from the left-most stitch, knit into the right-most stitch and continue knitting the row. Slide the work to the right end of the dpn and continue the process until 40 I-cord rows are knit, tugging at the cord occasionally to straighten. Then begin increases to make earflap.

Row 1 (WS): Knit.

Row 2 (RS): K1, m1L, k2, m1L, k1—6 sts.

Row 3: Knit.

Row 4: K1, m1L, k4, m1L, k1—8 sts.

Row 5: Knit.

Row 6: K1, m1L, k6, m1L, k1—10 sts.

Row 7: Knit.

Row 8: K1, m1L, k8, m1L, k1—12 sts.

Row 9: Knit.

Row 10: K1, m1L, k10, m1L, k1—14 sts.

Row 11: Knit.

Row 12: K1, m1L, k12, m1L, k1—16 sts.

Row 13: Knit.

Row 14: K1, m1L, k14, m1L, k1—18 sts.

Rows 15–19: Knit.

Cut yarn, leaving 8" (20.5 cm) tail for weaving in.

Sophisti-Cat

A stunning knit, this square hat is a paradox. Both sophisticated in style and whimsical with its pointy cat-ear corners, this hat speaks to our grown-up selves without giving up on our playful sides!

FINISHED MEASUREMENTS
Circumference at brim band 17" (43 cm) unstretched, 8" (20 cm) in length from brim edge to crown; will fit head circumference of 20" to 23" (50.5 to 58 cm)

YARN
130 yds (119 m) bulky weight #5 yarn (shown knitted in #6188 Indigo, Berroco Vintage Chunky, 52% acrylic, 40% wool, 8% nylon, 136 yds/125 m per skein)

NEEDLES AND OTHER MATERIALS
- One 16" (40.5 cm) circular knitting needle US 9 (5.5 mm) or size needed to obtain gauge
- One size US 9 (5.5 mm) double-pointed needle or size needed to obtain gauge
- Cable needle
- Stitch marker
- Scissors
- Yarn needle

GAUGE
16 sts x 20 rows in cable pattern = 4" (10 cm) square

SPECIAL STITCHES
2/2 Left Purl Cross (2/2 LPC): Slip next 2 sts to cable needle, hold cable needle to front of work, purl 2 sts from main needle, knit 2 sts from cable needle.

2/2 Right Purl Cross (2/2 RPC): Slip next 2 sts to cable needle, hold cable needle to back of work, knit 2 sts from main needle, purl 2 sts from cable needle.

2/2 Left Cross (2/2 LC): Slip next 2 sts to cable needle, hold cable needle to front of work, knit 2 sts from main needle, knit 2 sts from cable needle.

Note

- Hat is worked in rounds from bottom edge to top seam. The hat will be seamed from the outside with a three-needle bind-off.
- For photo tutorials on the cable stitches and three-needle bind-off, see pages 114–117 and 130–131.
- See page 8 for the charts for the Brim and the Body Cable Pattern.

2/2 Right Cross (2/2 RC): Slip next 2 sts to cable needle, hold cable needle to back of work, knit 2 sts from main needle, knit 2 sts from cable needle

Cast On

Using long-tail method and circular needle, CO 76 sts. Place a stitch marker between first and last sts and join in the round, being careful not to twist the cast-on row.

Brim

Rnds 1–2: [P8, (k2, p2) 6 times, p6] twice.
Rnds 3–4: [K10, (p2, k2) 5 times, k8] twice.
Rnds 5–6: [P8, (k2, p2) 6 times, p6] twice.
Rnd 7: [K9, (k1, p2, k1) twice, kfb, p1, pfb, (k2, p2) twice, k10] twice—80 sts.
Rnd 8: [K10, (p2, [k2, p2] twice) twice, k10] twice.

Body

Rnd 1: [P8, (k2, p2) twice, 2/2 LPC, 2/2 RPC, (p2, k2) twice, p8] twice.
Rnd 2: [P8, k2, p2, (k2, p4, k2) twice, p2, k2, p8] twice.
Rnd 3: [K8, (k2, p2) twice, p2, 2/2 LC, p2, (p2, k2) twice, k8] twice.
Rnd 4: [K10, p2, (k2, p4, k2) twice, p2, k10] twice.
Rnd 5: [P8, k2, p2, (2/2 LPC, 2/2 RPC) twice, p2, k2, p8] twice.
Rnd 6: [P8, (k2, p4, k2) 3 times, p8] twice.
Rnd 7: [K10, (p4, 2/2 RC) twice, p4, k10] twice.
Rnd 8: [K10, (p4, k4) 3 times, k6] twice.
Rnd 9: [P8, k2, p2, (2/2 RPC, 2/2 LPC) twice, p2, k2, p8] twice.
Rnd 10: [P8, k2, p2, (k2, p4, k2) twice, p2, k2, p8] twice.
Rnd 11: [K8, (k2, p2) twice, p2, 2/2 LC, p2, (p2, k2) twice, k8] twice.
Rnd 12: [K10, p2, (k2, p4, k2) twice, p2, k10] twice.
Rnd 13: [P8, k2, p2, (2/2 LPC, 2/2 RPC) twice, p2, k2, p8] twice.
Rnd 14: [P8, (k2, p4, k2) 3 times, p8] twice.
Rnd 15: [K10, (p4, 2/2 RC) twice, p4, k10] twice.

Rnd 16: [K10, (p4, k4) 3 times, k6] twice.
Rnd 17: [P8, k2, p2, (2/2 RPC, 2/2 LPC) twice, p2, k2, p8] twice.
Rnd 18: [P8, k2, p2, (k2, p4, k2) twice, p2, k2, p8] twice.
Rnd 19: [K8, (k2, p2) twice, p2, 2/2 LC, p2, (p2, k2) twice, k8] twice.
Rnd 20: [K10, p2, (k2, p4, k2) twice, p2, k10] twice.
Rnds 21–22: [P8, k2, p2, (k2, p4, k2) twice, p2, k2, p8] twice.
Rnd 23: [K8, (k2, p2) twice, p2, 2/2 LC, p2, (p2, k2) twice, k8] twice.
Rnd 24: [K10, p2, (k2, p4, k2) twice, p2, k10] twice.
Rnd 25: [P8, (k2, p2) twice, 2/2 RPC, 2/2 LPC, (p2, k2) twice, p8] twice.
Rnd 26: [P4, (p2, [p2, k2] 3 times) twice, p8] twice.
Rnds 27–28: [K10, (p2, [k2, p2] twice) twice, k10] twice.
Rnds 29–30: [P4, (p2, [p2, k2] 3 times) twice, p8] twice.
Rnd 31: [K10, (p2, k2) twice, p2tog twice, (k2, p2) twice, k10] twice—76 sts.
Rnd 32: [K10, (p2, k2) 5 times, k8] twice.
Rnds 33–34: [P8, (k2, p2) 6 times, p6] twice.
Rnds 35–36: [K10, (p2, k2) 5 times, k8] twice.
Rnds 37–38: [P8, (k2, p2) 6 times, p6] twice.

Finishing

Work a three-needle bind-off across top edge. Cut yarn, leaving an 8" (20.5 cm) tail. Feed tail through remaining loop, and tighten. Weave in yarn tails on inside of hat.

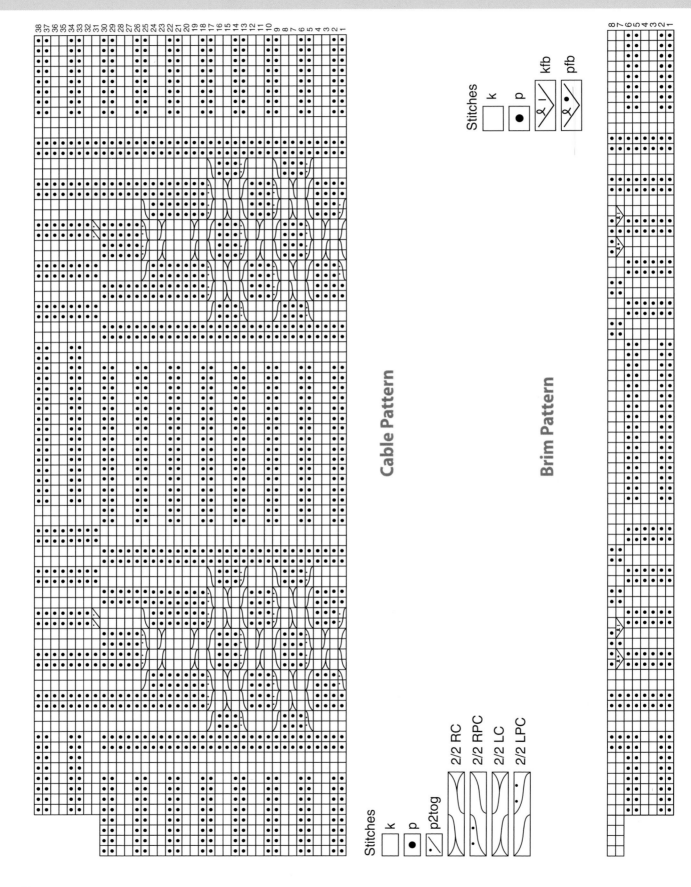

Cable Pattern

Brim Pattern

Stitches

k

p

kfb

pfb

Stitches

k

p

p2tog

2/2 RC

2/2 RPC

2/2 LC

2/2 LPC

Portsmouth Watchman

Arhythmical pattern that packs a toasty punch! Much like thermal clothing, this waffled design traps in body heat, keeping you cozy. Knitted extra long, this hat can be folded over for a double insulated layer.

Knit in Bright Orange

FINISHED MEASUREMENTS

S/M: Circumference at brim band 16" (41 cm) unstretched, 11" (28 cm) in length from brim edge to crown; will fit head circumference of 20" to 21" (50.5 to 53 cm)

L/XL: Circumference at brim band 17" (43 cm) unstretched, 12" (30 cm) in length from brim edge to crown; will fit head circumference of 22" to 23" (56 to 58 cm)

YARN

S/M: 135 yds (123 m) bulky weight #5 yarn (shown knitted in #0002 Bright Orange, Willow Yarns Daily Bulky, 100% superwash wool, 106 yds/97 m per skein)

L/XL: 150 yds (137 m) bulky weight #5 yarn (shown knitted in #0014 Lodestone, Willow Yarns Daily Bulky, 100% superwash wool, 106 yds/97 m per skein)

NEEDLES AND OTHER MATERIALS

- **S/M:** One 16" (40.5 cm) circular knitting needle US 10 (6 mm) or size needed to obtain gauge, US 10 (6 mm) set of 5 double-pointed needles or size needed to obtain gauge
- **L/XL:** One 16" (40.5 cm) circular knitting needle US 10.5 (6.5 mm) or size needed to obtain gauge, US 10.5 (6.5 mm) set of 5 double-pointed needles or size needed to obtain gauge
- Stitch marker
- Scissors
- Yarn needle

Note

- Pattern instructions are the same throughout for both sizes; the only difference is the needle size.
- Hat is worked in rounds from bottom edge to crown. Switch from circular needles to double-pointed needles when necessary during crown shaping.

GAUGE

S/M: Using US 10 (6 mm) needles, 14 sts x 18 rows in Mistake Rib patt = 4" (10 cm) square

L/XL: Using US 10.5 (6.5 mm) needles, 12 sts x 16 rows in Mistake Rib patt = 4" (10 cm) square

STITCH PATTERN

Mistake Rib Pattern

Rnd 1: *K2, p2; rep from * around.

Rnd 2: K1 *p2, k2; rep from * around until the last 3 stitches; p2, k1.

Cast On

Using long-tail method and circular needle, CO 60 sts. Place a stitch marker between first and last sts and join in the round, being careful not to twist the cast-on row.

Brim and Body

Rnds 1–60: Work Mistake Rib patt 30 times.

Crown Shaping

Rnd 1: *Sl1, k2tog, psso; rep from * around—20 sts.

Rnd 2: *K2tog; rep from * around—10 sts.

Finishing

Cut yarn, leaving an 8" (20.5 cm) tail. Thread yarn needle with end and pick up remaining stitches on knitting needles. Pull tightly to close and secure end. Weave in yarn tail on inside of hat.

Knit in Lodestone

Trapper

This charming faux fur-lined hat is reminiscent of the Russian ushanka, meaning "ear hat". The flaps provide additional coverage from the elements for your ears and jaw. A creamy colored acrylic yarn mimics shearling fleece, coupled with a deep aubergine purple for maximum contrast. Finish off with handmade wooden buttons for a rustic look.

FINISHED MEASUREMENTS

Circumference at brim band 20" (50.5 cm) unstretched, 8" (20 cm) in length from brim edge to crown, 13" (33 cm) in length from ear flap edge to crown; will fit head circumference of 20" to 23" (50.5 to 58 cm)

YARN

Main Color (MC): 100 yds (91 m) super bulky weight #6 yarn (shown knitted in #640-147 Eggplant, Lion Brand Wool-Ease Thick & Quick, 80% acrylic, 20% wool, 106 yds/97 m per skein)

Contrasting Color (CC): 30 yds (27 m) super bulky weight #6 yarn (shown knitted in #068048 Café Au Lait, Coats and Clark Red Heart Light & Lofty, 100% acrylic, 140 yds/128 m per skein)

NEEDLES AND OTHER MATERIALS

- One 16" (40.5 cm) circular knitting needle US 13 (9 mm) or size needed to obtain gauge
- US 13 (9 mm) set of 5 double-pointed needles or size needed to obtain gauge.
- Stitch marker
- US K-10$^{1/2}$ (6.5 mm) crochet hook
- Scissors
- Yarn needle
- Two $^{7}/_{8}$" (2.25 cm) buttons

GAUGE

9 sts x 12 rows in stockinette stitch = 4" (10 cm) square

- Knit front flap first in CC, then 2 ear flaps in MC, with double-pointed needles, then incorporate into the cast-on round to complete hat.
- Switch from circular needle to double-pointed needles when necessary during crown shaping.
- For a photo tutorial on backward loop cast-on, see page 107.

Hat

Using the circular needle, cast on by purling across 14 sts of WS of front flap, then knit across 10 sts of RS of one earflap, CO 6 sts using the backward loop method, knit across 10 sts of RS of second earflap. Place a stitch marker between first and last sts and join in the round, being careful not to twist cast-on row.

Rnds 1–18: Knit—40 sts.

Crown Shaping

Rnd 1: *K3, k2tog; rep from * around—32 sts.
Rnd 2: Knit.
Rnd 3: *K2, k2tog; rep from * around—24 sts.
Rnd 4: Knit.
Rnd 5: *K1, k2tog; rep from * around—16 sts.
Rnd 6: Knit.
Rnd 7: *K2tog; rep from * around—8 sts.

Finishing

Cut yarn, leaving an 8" (20.5 cm) tail. Thread yarn needle with end and pick up remaining stitches on knitting needles. Pull tightly to close and secure end. Fold front flap up and affix two buttons to top corners to secure into place. Beginning at back of hat, use crochet hook to single crochet with CC around entire edge of hat. Weave in yarn tails on inside of hat.

Front Flap

Using long-tail method and 2 dpns, CO 14 sts using CC.
Rows 1 (WS)–12: Knit.
Cut yarn, leaving an 8" (20.5 cm) tail.

Earflap (make 2)

Using long-tail method and 2 dpns, CO 4 sts using MC.
Row 1 (WS): Purl.
Row 2: K1, m1L, k2, m1L, k1—6 sts.
Row 3: Purl.
Row 4: K1, m1L, k4, m1L, k1—8 sts.
Row 5: Purl.
Row 6: K1, m1L, k6, m1L, k1—10 sts.
Odd Rows 7–17: K2, p6, k2
Even Rows 8–16: Knit.
Cut yarn, leaving an 8" (20.5 cm) tail.

Steps & Ladders

This dramatic knit is roomy and comfortable, and the zigzag design is deceptively easy. Quick to knit, it is the ideal last-minute gift hat.

FINISHED MEASUREMENTS

Circumference at brim band 19" (48 cm) unstretched, 10" (25 cm) in length from brim edge to crown; will fit head circumference of 20" to 23" (50.5 to 58 cm)

YARN

150 yds (137 m) bulky weight #5 yarn (shown knitted in SS543 Reed, Brown Sheep Company Shepherd's Shades, 100% wool, 131 yds/118 m per skein)

NEEDLES AND OTHER MATERIALS

- One 16" (40.5 cm) circular knitting needle US 10 (6 mm) or size needed to obtain gauge
- US 10 (6 mm) set of 5 double-pointed needles or size needed to obtain gauge
- Stitch marker
- Scissors
- Yarn needle

GAUGE

13 sts x 20 rows in stitch pattern = 4" (10 cm) square

STITCH PATTERN

Rnds 1–2: *K1, p1, k1, p5; rep from * around.
Rnds 3–4: *K1, p1, k5, p1; rep from * around.
Rnds 5–6: *K1, p5, k1, p1; rep from * around.
Rnds 7–8: *K5, p1, k1, p1; rep from * around.
Rnds 9–10: P4, *k1, p1, k1, p5; rep from *, until the last 4; k1, p1, k1, p1.
Rnds 11–12: K3, *p1, k1, p1, k5; rep from *, until the last 5; p1, k1, p1, k2.
Rnds 13–14: P2, *k1, p1, k1, p5; rep from *, until the last 6; k1, p1, k1, p3.
Rnds 15–16: K1, *p1, k1, p1, k5; rep from *, until the last 7; p1, k1, p1, k4.

- Hat is worked in rounds from bottom edge to crown. Switch from circular needles to double-pointed needles when necessary during crown shaping.

Cast On

Using long-tail method and circular needle, CO 72 sts. Place a stitch marker between first and last sts and join in the round, being careful not to twist the cast-on row.

Brim

Rnds 1–2: Purl.
Rnds 3–4: Knit.
Rnds 5–6: Purl.
Rnds 7–8: Knit.

Body

Rnds 1–48: Work entire stitch pattern 3 times.

Crown Shaping

Rnd 1: *K1, p1, k1, p2tog, p3; rep from * around—63 sts.
Rnd 2: *K1, p1, k1, p4; rep from * around.
Rnd 3: *K1, p1, k2tog, k2, p1; rep from * around—54 sts.
Rnd 4: *K1, p1, k3, p1; rep from * around.
Rnd 5: *K1, p2tog, p1, k1, p1; rep from * around—45 sts.
Rnd 6: *K1, p2, k1, p1; rep from * around.
Rnd 7: *K2tog, p1, k1, p1; rep from * around—36 sts.
Rnd 8: *K1, p1; rep from * around.
Rnd 9: *K2tog; rep from * around—18 sts.
Rnd 10: *K2tog; rep from * around—9 sts.

Finishing

Cut yarn, leaving an 8" (20.5 cm) tail. Thread yarn needle with end and pick up remaining stitches on knitting needles. Pull tightly to close and secure end. Weave in yarn tails on inside of hat.

Sidewinder

This hat is a nice departure from hats knit in the round. It uses a crochet provisional cast-on and Kitchener stitch seaming to graft an almost undetectable join. If these techniques are not in your wheelhouse, try a long-tail cast on and traditional bind-off, then sew the seam up from the inside.

FINISHED MEASUREMENTS
Circumference at brim band 16" (41 cm) unstretched, 12" (30 cm) in length from brim edge to crown; will fit head circumference of 20" to 23" (50.5 to 58 cm)

YARN
140 yds (128 m) bulky weight #5 yarn (shown knitted in #753-206 Woodlands, Lion Brand Tweed Stripes, 100% acrylic, 144 yds/132 m per skein)

NEEDLES AND OTHER MATERIALS
- US 10 (6 mm) set of 2 straight needles or size to obtain gauge
- US J-10 (6 mm) crochet hook
- Scrap yarn
- Scissors
- Yarn needle

GAUGE
14.5 sts x 18 rows in garter stitch = 4" (10 cm) square

STITCH PATTERN
Short-Row Wedge
Row 1: Knit 34, turn.
Row 2: Knit 20, turn.
Row 3: Knit 26, turn.
Row 4: Knit 40, turn.
Row 5: Knit 34, turn.
Row 6: Knit 34, turn.

- Hat is knit flat in short-row wedges, beginning with a provisional cast-on, then seamed with Kitchener stitch.
- For photo tutorials on provisional crochet cast-on and Kitchener stitch, see pages 107 and 131.

Cast On

Using scrap yarn, the crochet hook, and one of your needles, CO 40 sts using provisional crochet cast-on. Crochet 4 chain sts after cast-on row to easily unravel scrap yarn later. Switch to working yarn and knit first row into live sts on needle.

Body

Rows 1–150: Work entire Short-Row Wedge patt 25 times.

Finishing

Break yarn, leaving 14" (36 cm) tail. Untie provisional cast-on row scrap yarn and, using free needle, pick up the live stitches from provisional cast-on row. Remove scrap yarn. Be sure both needles are pointing to the right and that the wrong sides of the knitted fabric are facing each other. Thread yarn needle with tail and Kitchener stitch the live stitches together from brim to crown.

Continue until one stitch on each knitting needle remains. Run your yarn needle through both of them and pick up the top-edge row of stitches at crown. Draw together to close and secure end. Weave in yarn tails on inside of hat.

Cozy Cable

entle flowing cables create a sculptured fitted hat, leading to a graceful crown. These cables are straightforward and ideal for a knitter new to cables. The pattern provides sizing for a smaller and larger version.

FINISHED MEASUREMENTS

S/M: Circumference at brim band 16" (41 cm) unstretched, 8.5" (22 cm) in length from brim edge to crown; will fit head circumference of 20" to 21" (50.5 to 53 cm)

L/XL: Circumference at brim band 17" (43 cm) unstretched, 9" (23 cm) in length from brim edge to crown; will fit head circumference of 22" to 23" (56 to 58 cm)

YARN

S/M: 155 yds (142 m) worsted weight #4 yarn (shown knitted in #363543 Burgundy, Lion Brand Vanna's Choice Worsted, 100% premium acrylic, 170 yds/156 m per skein)

L/XL: 170 yds (156 m) worsted weight #4 yarn (shown knitted in #324796 Honey, Lion Brand Vanna's Choice Worsted, 100% premium acrylic, 170 yds/156 m per skein)

NEEDLES AND OTHER MATERIALS

- **S/M:** One 16" (40.5 cm) circular knitting needle US 8 (5 mm) or size needed to obtain gauge, US 8 (5 mm) set of 5 double-pointed needles or size needed to obtain gauge
- **L/XL:** One 16" (40.5 cm) circular knitting needle US 9 (5.5 mm) or size needed to obtain gauge, US 9 (5.5 mm) set of 5 double-pointed needles or size needed to obtain gauge
- Stitch marker
- Cable needle
- Scissors
- Yarn needle

GAUGE

S/M: Using US 8 (5 mm) needle, 18 sts x 24 rows in stitch pattern = 4" (10 cm) square

L/XL: Using US 9 (5.5 mm) needle, 20 sts x 26 rows in stitch pattern = 4" (10 cm) square

Note

- To achieve different sizes, different needle sizes are used and more increases are worked for the L/XL.
- Hat is worked in rounds from bottom edge to crown. Switch from circular needles to double-pointed needles when necessary during crown shaping.
- For photo tutorials on 3/3 Left Cross and 3/3 Right Cross, see page 118.

SPECIAL STITCHES

3/3 Left Cross (3/3 LC): Slip next 3 sts to cable needle, hold cable needle to front of work, knit 3 sts from main needle, knit 3 sts from cable needle

3/3 Right Cross (3/3 RC): Slip next 3 sts to cable needle, hold cable needle to back of work, knit 3 sts from main needle, knit 3 sts from cable needle

STITCH PATTERN

Rnd 1: *3/3 LC, k6; rep from * around.
Rnds 2–4: Knit.
Rnd 5: *K6, 3/3 RC; rep from * around.
Rnds 6–8: Knit.

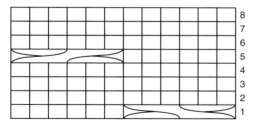

Stitches

☐ k
3/3 RC
3/3 LC

Cast On

Using long-tail method and circular needle, CO 84 sts. Place a stitch marker between first and last sts and join in the round, being careful not to twist the cast-on row.

Brim

Rnds 1–8: *K1, p1; rep from * around.

Increase

Increase for S/M version only
Rnd 9: *K7, m1L; rep from * around—96 sts.

Increase for L/XL version only
Rnd 9: *K3, m1L, k4, m1L; rep from * around—108 sts.

Body

Rnds 1–2: Knit.
Rnds 3–34: Work entire stitch pattern 4 times.

Crown Shaping

Rnd 1: *3/3 LC, k4, k2tog; rep from * around—88 (99) sts.
Rnd 2: Knit.
Rnd 3: *K9, k2tog; rep from * around—80 (90) sts.
Rnd 4: Knit.
Rnd 5: *K8, k2tog; rep from * around—72 (81) sts.
Rnd 6: Knit.
Rnd 7: *K7, k2tog; rep from * around—64 (72) sts.
Rnd 8: Knit.
Rnd 9: *3/3 RC, k2tog; rep from * around—56 (63) sts.
Rnd 10: Knit.
Rnd 11: *K5, k2tog; rep from * around—48 (54) sts.
Rnd 12: Knit.
Rnd 13: *K4, k2tog; rep from * around—40 (45) sts.
Rnd 14: Knit.
Rnd 15: *K3, k2tog; rep from * around—32 (36) sts.
Rnd 16: Knit.
Rnd 17: *K2tog; rep from * around—16 (18) sts.

Finishing

Cut yarn, leaving an 8" (20.5 cm) tail. Thread yarn needle with end and pick up remaining stitches on knitting needles. Pull tightly to close and secure end. Weave in yarn tails on inside of hat.

Greenwich

Knit this hat in a thin worsted yarn for a lightweight and trendy slouch cap, perfect for sweeping up your tresses on those bad hair days. A self-striping yarn adds visual interest to what will undoubtedly be a go-to favorite in your wardrobe.

FINISHED MEASUREMENTS

S/M: Circumference at brim band 20" (51 cm) unstretched, 10" (25 cm) in length from brim edge to crown; will fit head circumference of 20" to 21" (50.5 to 53 cm)

L/XL: Circumference at brim band 22" (56 cm) unstretched, 11" (28 cm) in length from brim edge to crown; will fit head circumference of 22" to 23" (56 to 58 cm)

YARN

S/M: 180 yds (165 m) worsted weight #4 yarn (shown knitted in #060504 Gamut, Bernat Mosaic, 100% acrylic, 209 yds/191 m per skein)

L/XL: 200 yds (183 m) worsted weight #4 yarn (shown knitted in #435269 Waterfall, Bernat Mosaic, 100% acrylic, 209 yds/191 m per skein)

NEEDLES AND OTHER MATERIALS

- **S/M:** One 16" (40.5 cm) circular knitting needle US 7 (4.5 mm) or size needed to obtain gauge, US 7 (4.5 mm) set of 5 double-pointed needles or size needed to obtain gauge
- **L/XL:** One 16" (40.5 cm) circular knitting needle US 8 (5 mm) or size needed to obtain gauge, US 8 (5 mm) set of 5 double-pointed needles or size needed to obtain gauge
- Stitch marker
- Scissors
- Yarn needle

GAUGE

S/M: Using US 7 (4.5 mm) needle, 20 sts x 26 rows in stockinette stitch = 4" (10 cm) square

L/XL: Using US 8 (5 mm) needle, 18 sts x 24 rows in stockinette stitch = 4" (10 cm) square

Knit in Gamut

Knit in Waterfall

Cast On

Using long-tail method and circular needle, CO 84 sts.
Place a stitch marker between first and last sts and join
in the round, being careful not to twist the cast-on row.

Brim

Rnd 1: Purl.
Rnds 2–12: Knit.
Rnd 13: Purl.

- Pattern instructions are the same throughout for both sizes; the only difference is the needle size.
- Hat is worked in rounds from bottom edge to crown. Switch from circular needles to double-pointed needles when necessary during crown shaping.

Rnds 14–24: Knit.
Rnd 25: Purl.
Rnds 26–36: Knit.
Rnd 37: Purl.

Body

Rnd 1: *K11, kfb; rep from * around—91 sts.
Rnd 2: Knit.
Rnd 3: *K12, kfb; rep from * around—98 sts.
Rnd 4: Knit.
Rnd 5: *K13, kfb; rep from * around—105 sts.
Rnd 6: Knit.
Rnd 7: *K14, kfb; rep from * around—112 sts.
Rnd 8: Knit.
Rnd 9: *K15, kfb; rep from * around—119 sts.
Rnd 10: Knit.
Rnd 11: *K16, kfb; rep from * around—126 sts.
Rnd 12: Purl.
Rnds 13–23: Knit.
Rnd 24: Purl.

Crown Shaping

Rnd 1: *K5, k2tog; rep from * around—108 sts.
Rnd 2: Knit.
Rnd 3: *K4, k2tog; rep from * around—90 sts.
Rnd 4: Knit.
Rnd 5: *K3, k2tog; rep from * around—72 sts.
Rnd 6: Knit.
Rnd 7: *K2, k2tog; rep from * around—54 sts.
Rnd 8: Knit.
Rnd 9: *K1, k2tog; rep from * around—36 sts.
Rnd 10: Knit.
Rnd 11: *K2tog; rep from * around—18 sts.

Finishing

Cut yarn, leaving an 8" (20.5 cm) tail. Thread yarn needle
with end and pick up remaining stitches on knitting
needles. Pull tightly to close and secure end. Weave in
yarn tails on inside of hat.

Slalom

A staple in any ski lodge, the Slalom beanie is a comfortable argyle knit hat with a slightly puckered crown. Knitting through the back loop of the brim band ribbing makes for a twisted stitch with an etched quality. The stylized argyle pattern is classic and playful.

FINISHED MEASUREMENTS

Circumference at brim band 17" (43 cm) unstretched, 9" (23 cm) in length from brim edge to crown; will fit head circumference of 20" to 23" (50.5 to 58 cm)

YARN

Color A: 150 yds (137 m) worsted weight #4 yarn (shown knitted in #06 Dark Grey, Valley Yarns Northampton, 100% wool, 247 yds/226 m per skein)

Color B: 60 yds (55 m) worsted weight #4 yarn (shown knitted in #01 White, Valley Yarns Northampton, 100% wool, 247 yds/226 m per skein)

Color C: 50 yds (46 m) worsted weight #4 yarn (shown knitted in #17 Red, Valley Yarns Northampton, 100% wool, 247 yds/226 m per skein)

NEEDLES AND OTHER MATERIALS

- One 16" (40.5 cm) circular knitting needle US 7 (4.5 mm) or size needed to obtain gauge
- One US 7 (4.5 mm) set of 5 double-pointed needles or size needed to obtain gauge
- Stitch marker
- Scissors
- Yarn needle

GAUGE

20 sts x 24 rows in stockinette stitch = 4" (10 cm) square

Note

- Hat is worked in rounds from bottom edge to crown. Switch from circular needles to double-pointed needles when necessary during crown shaping.
- Color charts are read from bottom to top and from right to left.
- Knitting a pattern in multiple colors is called stranding. Only one color is knit at a time, while the other colors will wait their turn and be carried behind the work until they are used again. Be certain that the carried yarns remain at a relaxed tension. To keep the inside of your work tidy when switching from one color to another, be consistent regarding which color strands are carried underneath or above the previous color. When working sections that do not include one of the colors, run this unworked color up the side of the work by twisting it with the main color used at the end of the round rather than cutting it and reattaching it each time it is needed.

Cast On

Using long-tail method and circular needle, CO 90 sts in Color A. Place a stitch marker between first and last sts and join in the round, being careful not to twist the cast-on row.

Brim

Rnds 1–8: *K1tbl, p1; rep from * around.
Rnd 9: *K3, m1; rep from * around—120 sts.

Body

Rnds 1–33: Working in stockinette stitch, follow the color chart below for 33 rnds, repeating the 20-stitch pattern around each round.

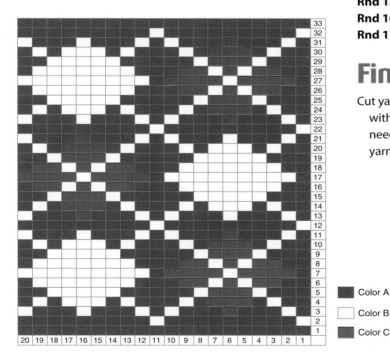

Crown Shaping

Using Color A:
Rnd 1: *K8, k2tog; rep from * around—108 sts.
Rnd 2: Knit.
Rnd 3: *K7, k2tog; rep from * around—96 sts.
Rnd 4: Knit.
Rnd 5: *K6, k2tog; rep from * around—84 sts.
Rnd 6: Knit.
Rnd 7: *K5, k2tog; rep from * around—72 sts.
Rnd 8: Knit.
Rnd 9: *K4, k2tog; rep from * around—60 sts.
Rnd 10: Knit.
Rnd 11: *K3, k2tog; rep from * around—48 sts.
Rnd 12: Knit.
Rnd 13: *K2, k2tog; rep from * around—36 sts.
Rnd 14: Knit.
Rnd 15: *K1, k2tog; rep from * around—24 sts.
Rnd 16: Knit.
Rnd 17: *K2tog; rep from * around—12 sts.

Finishing

Cut yarn, leaving an 8" (20.5 cm) tail. Thread yarn needle with end and pick up remaining stitches on knitting needles. Pull tightly to close and secure end. Weave in yarn tails on inside of hat.

- ■ Color A
- □ Color B
- ■ Color C

Spanish Moss

Love the look of knitted cables but not quite ready for something so fiddly? This mock cable pattern is just the thing! Basic lacework creates a serpentine cabled effect with ease.

FINISHED MEASUREMENTS

Circumference at brim band 18" (46 cm) unstretched, 10.5" (27 cm) in length from brim edge to crown; will fit head circumference of 20" to 23" (50.5 to 58 cm)

YARN

150 yds (137 m) bulky weight #5 yarn (shown knitted in #068325 Willow, Lion Brand Wool-Ease Chunky, 80% acrylic, 20% wool, 153 yds/140 m per skein)

NEEDLES AND OTHER MATERIALS

- One 16" (40.5 cm) circular knitting needle US 10.5 (6.5 mm) or size needed to obtain gauge
- US 10.5 (6.5 mm) set of 5 double-pointed needles or size needed to obtain gauge
- Stitch marker
- Scissors
- Yarn needle

GAUGE

14 sts x 18 rows in stitch pattern = 4" (10 cm) square

STITCH PATTERN

Rnd 1: *K1, yo, k1, p2; rep from * around—85 sts.
Rnds 2–3: *K3, p2; rep from * around.
Rnd 4: *Sl1, k2, psso, p2; rep from * around—68 sts.

Note

• Hat is worked in rounds from bottom edge to crown. Switch from circular needles to double-pointed needles when necessary during crown shaping.

Cast On

Using long-tail method and circular needle, CO 68 sts. Place a stitch marker between first and last sts and join in the round, being careful not to twist the cast-on row.

Brim

Rnds 1–8: *K2, p2; rep from * around.

Body

Rnds 1–36: Work entire stitch pattern 9 times.

Crown Shaping

Rnd 1: *K1, yo, k1, p2; rep from * around—85 sts.
Rnd 2: *K3, p2; rep from * around.
Rnd 3: *K1, k2tog, p2; rep from * around—68 sts.
Rnd 4: *Sl1, k1, psso, p2; rep from * around—51 sts.
Rnd 5: *K1, p2tog; rep from * around—34 sts.
Rnd 6: *K2tog; rep from * around—17 sts.

Finishing

Cut yarn, leaving an 8" (20.5 cm) tail. Thread yarn needle with end and pick up remaining stitches on knitting needles. Pull tightly to close and secure end. Weave in yarn tails on inside of hat.

Mariner

triking cable waves grown from the brim band spiral around this fitted beanie. Although an advanced technique, the unique cable crossover stitch is easy to learn and creates a stretchy knit. A deep cable needle is essential for this project.

FINISHED MEASUREMENTS
Circumference at brim band 16" (41 cm) unstretched, 9" (23 cm) in length from brim edge to crown; will fit head circumference of 20" to 23" (50.5 to 58 cm)

YARN
155 yds (142 m) worsted weight #4 yarn (shown knitted in #2510 Aquamarine, Stitch Nation By Debbie Stoller Full O' Sheep, 100% Peruvian wool, 155 yds/142 m per skein)

NEEDLES AND OTHER MATERIALS
- One 16" (40.5 cm) circular knitting needle US 8 (5 mm) or size needed to obtain gauge
- US 8 (5 mm) set of 5 double-pointed needles or size needed to obtain gauge
- Stitch marker
- Cable needle (one with a deep bend in it)
- Scissors
- Yarn needle

GAUGE
18 sts x 22 rows in stitch pattern = 4" (10 mm) square

SPECIAL STITCHES
6 Stitch Right Cable Crossover (6RCC):
Slip next 3 sts to cable needle, hold cable needle to back of work, knit next 2 sts. Replace purl st from cable needle back onto left hand needle and purl. Knit 2 sts on cable needle. Purl next st.

Note

- Hat is worked in rounds from bottom edge to crown. Switch from circular needles to double-pointed needles when necessary during crown shaping.
- For step-by-step photo-illustrated instructions for the 6 Stitch Right Cable Crossover, see page 120.

STITCH PATTERN

Rnds 1–4: *K2, p1; rep from * around.

Rnd 5: *K2, p1; rep from * around until last 3 sts. Slip 3 sts to right hand needle, remove stitch marker, replace 3 slipped sts to left hand needle, replace marker.

Rnd 6: *6RCC; rep from * around.

Rnd 7: Remove stitch marker. K2, p1. Replace stitch marker. *K2, P1; rep from * around.

Rnds 8–11: *K2, p1; rep from * around.

Rnd 12: *6RCC; rep from * around.

Cast On

Using long-tail method and circular needle, CO 96 sts. Place a stitch marker between first and last sts and join in the round, being careful not to twist the cast-on row.

Brim and Body

Rnds 1–48: Work entire stitch patt 4 times.

Rnds 49–54: Work rnds 1-6 of stitch patt.

Crown Shaping

Rnd 1: *K2, p1, k2, p1, k2, p1, k2tog, p1; rep from * around—88 sts.

Rnd 2: *K2, p1, k2, p1, k2tog, p1, k1, p1; rep from * around—80 sts.

Rnd 3: *K2, p1, K2tog, p1, k1, p1, k1, p1; rep from * around—72 sts.

Rnd 4: *K2tog, p1, k1, p1, k1, p1, k1, p1; rep from * around—64 sts.

Rnd 5: *K2tog, k1, p1; rep from * around—48 sts.

Rnd 6: *K1, k2tog; rep from * around—32 sts.

Rnd 7: *K2tog; rep from * around—16 sts.

Finishing

Cut yarn, leaving an 8" (20.5 cm) tail. Thread yarn needle with end and pick up remaining stitches on knitting needles. Pull tightly to close and secure end. Weave in yarn tails on inside of hat.

Helmet

Charming in its simplicity, this hat can easily be personalized. Use complementary or contrasting colors, adorn with a pom-pom, or add braids to the ends of the ear flaps.

FINISHED MEASUREMENTS

Circumference at brim band 20" (51 cm) unstretched, 8" (20 cm) in length from brim edge to crown; will fit head circumference of 20" to 23" (50.5 to 58 cm)

YARN

Color A: 50 yds (46 m) super bulky weight #6 yarn (shown knitted in #640-124 Barley, Lion Brand Wool-Ease Thick & Quick, 80% acrylic, 20% wool, 106 yds/97 m per skein)

Color B: 50 yds (46 m) super bulky weight #6 yarn (shown knitted in #640-099 Fisher-man, Lion Brand Wool-Ease Thick & Quick, 80% acrylic, 20% wool, 106 yds/97 m per skein)

NEEDLES AND OTHER MATERIALS

- One 16" (40.5 cm) circular knitting needle US 13 (9 mm) or size needed to obtain gauge
- US 13 (9 mm) set of 5 double-pointed needles or size needed to obtain gauge.
- Stitch marker
- Scissors
- Yarn needle

GAUGE

9 sts x 12 rows in stockinette stitch = 4" (10 cm) square

Note

- Knit two ear flaps onto double-pointed needles, then incorporate into the cast-on round on circular needle.
- Switch from circular needle back to double-pointed needles when necessary during crown shaping.
- For a photo tutorial on backward loop cast-on, see page 107).

Brim

Rnd 1: Purl—40 sts.
Rnd 2: Knit.
Rnds 3–12: Repeat rnds 1 and 2 five times.
Rnd 13: Purl.

Body

Cut Color A, leaving an 8" (20.5 cm) tail for weaving in. Pick up Color B.
Rnds 1–10: Knit.

Crown Shaping

Rnd 1: *K3, k2tog; rep from * around—32 sts.
Rnd 2: Knit.
Rnd 3: *K2, k2tog; rep from * around—24 sts.
Rnd 4: Knit.
Rnd 5: *K1, k2tog; rep from * around—16 sts.
Rnd 6: Knit.
Rnd 7: *K2tog; rep from * around—8 sts.

Finishing

Cut yarn, leaving an 8" (20.5 cm) tail. Thread yarn needle with end and pick up remaining stitches on knitting needles. Pull tightly to close and secure end. Weave in yarn tails on inside of hat.

Earflap (make 2)

Using long-tail method and 2 dpns, CO 3 sts in Color A.
Row 1 (WS): Knit.
Row 2 (RS): *K1, m1L, k1, m1L, k1—5 sts.
Row 3: Knit.
Row 4: *K1, m1L, k3, m1L, k1—7 sts.
Row 5: Knit.
Row 6: *K1, m1L, k5, m1L, k1—9 sts.
Row 7: Knit.
Row 8: *K1, m1L, k7, m1L, k1—11 sts.
Row 9: Knit.
Cut an 8" (20.5 cm) tail for weaving in.

Hat

Using long-tail method and circular needle, CO 3 sts with Color A. With RS facing, knit across one ear flap. Using the backward loop method, CO 12 sts. With RS facing, knit across second earflap. CO 3 sts with backward loop method. Place a stitch marker between first and last st and join in the round, being careful not to twist cast-on row.

Fairway

I n golf, the fairway refers to the short-cut grassy area between the tee box and putting green. This elegant beret uses slipped stitches over a reverse stockinette background to point the way to that hole in one at the center point of the crown. The next pattern, the Mulligan, takes the idea one step further by adding a peaked brim visor.

FINISHED MEASUREMENTS

S/M: Circumference at brim band 20" (51 cm) unstretched, 8" (20 cm) in length from brim edge to crown; will fit head circumference of 20" to 21" (50.5 to 53 cm)

L/XL: Circumference at brim band 22" (56 cm) unstretched, 8.5" (22 cm) in length from brim edge to crown; will fit head circumference of 22" to 23" (56 to 58 cm)

YARN

S/M: 100 yds (91 m) bulky weight #5 yarn, (shown knitted in #6631 Clover, Berroco Blackstone Tweed Chunky, 65% wool, 25% superkid mohair, 10% angora rabbit hair, 60 yds/55 m per skein)

L/XL: 120 yds (110 m) bulky weight #5 yarn

NEEDLES AND OTHER MATERIALS

- **S/M:** One 16" (40.5 cm) circular knitting needle US 10 (6 mm) or size needed to obtain gauge, US 10 (6 mm) set of 5 double-pointed needles or size needed to obtain gauge
- **L/XL:** One 16" (40.5 cm) circular knitting needle US 10.5 (6.5 mm) or size needed to obtain gauge, US 10.5 (6.5 mm) set of 5 double-pointed needles or size needed to obtain gauge
- Stitch marker
- Scissors
- Yarn needle

GAUGE

S/M: Using US 10 (6 cm) needles, 15 sts x 19 rows in reverse stockinette = 4" (10 cm) square

L/XL: Using US 10.5 (6.5 cm), 13 sts x 17 rows in reverse stockinette = 4" (10 cm) square

Note

- Pattern instructions are the same throughout for both sizes; the only difference is the needle size.
- Hat is worked in rounds from bottom edge to crown. Switch from circular needles to double-pointed needles when necessary during crown shaping.
- Berroco Blackstone Tweed Chunky is a somewhat delicate fiber. Be certain to avoid excessive tugging at this yarn to minimize breakage.

Cast On

Using long-tail method and circular needle, CO 60 sts. Place a stitch marker between first and last sts and join in the round, being careful not to twist the cast-on row.

Brim

Rnd 1: Knit.
Rnd 2: Purl.
Rnd 3: Knit.
Rnd 4: Purl.
Rnd 5: Knit.

Body

Rnd 1: *P5, sl1k; rep from * around.
Rnd 2: *P5, k1; rep from * around.
Rnd 3: *P1, m1P, p4, sl1k; rep from * around—70 sts.
Rnd 4: *P6, k1; rep from * around.
Rnd 5: *P1, m1P, p5, sl1k; rep from * around—80 sts.
Rnd 6: *P7, k1; rep from * around.
Rnd 7: *P1, m1P, p6, sl1k; rep from * around—90 sts.
Rnd 8: *P8, k1; rep from * around.
Rnd 9: *P1, m1P, p7, sl1k; rep from * around—100 sts.
Even Rnds 10–22: *P9, k1; rep from * around.
Odd Rnds 11–21: *P9, sl1k; rep from * around.

Crown Shaping

Rnd 1: *P1, p2tog, p6, sl1k; rep from * around—90 sts.
Rnd 2: *P8, k1; rep from * around.
Rnd 3: *P1, p2tog, p5, sl1k; rep from * around—80 sts.
Rnd 4: *P7, k1; rep from * around.
Rnd 5: *P1, p2tog, p4, sl1k; rep from * around—70 sts.
Rnd 6: *P6, k1; rep from * around.
Rnd 7: *P1, p2tog, p3, sl1k; rep from * around—60 sts.
Rnd 8: *P5, k1; rep from * around.
Rnd 9: *P1, p2tog, p2, sl1k; rep from * around—50 sts.
Rnd 10: *P4, k1; rep from * around.
Rnd 11: *P1, p2tog, p1, sl1k; rep from * around—40 sts.
Rnd 12: *P3, k1; rep from * around.
Rnd 13: *P1, p2tog, sl1k; rep from * around—30 sts.
Rnd 14: *P2, k1; rep from * around.
Rnd 15: *P2tog, sl1k; rep from * around—20 sts.
Rnd 16: *P1, k1; rep from * around.
Rnd 17: *K2tog; rep from * around—10 sts.

Finishing

Cut yarn, leaving an 8" (20.5 cm) tail. Thread yarn needle with end and pick up remaining stitches on knitting needles. Pull tightly to close and secure end. Weave in yarn tails on inside of hat.

Mulligan

Much like the golf stroke second shot it was named after, the Mulligan is the sequel to the previous pattern, Fairway. A sturdy peaked visor is knit separately and sewn to the edge of the brim to complete this vintage style golf cap.

FINISHED MEASUREMENTS

S/M: Circumference at brim band 20" (51 cm) unstretched, 8" (20 cm) in length from brim edge to crown; will fit head circumference of 20" to 21" (50.5 to 53 cm)

L/XL: Circumference at brim band 22" (56 cm) unstretched, 8.5" (22 cm) in length from brim edge to crown; will fit head circumference of 22" to 23" (56 to 58 cm)

YARN

S/M: 180 yds (165 m) bulky weight #5 yarn (shown knitted in #6658 Pitch, Berroco Blackstone Tweed Chunky, 65% wool, 25% superkid mohair, 10% angora rabbit hair, 60 yds/55 m per skein)

L/XL: 200 yds (183 m) bulky weight #5 yarn

NEEDLES AND OTHER MATERIALS

- **S/M:** One 16" (40.5 cm) circular knitting needle size US 10 (6 mm) or size needed to obtain gauge, US 10 (6 mm) set of 5 double-pointed needles or size needed to obtain gauge
- **L/XL:** One 16" (40.5 cm) circular knitting needle size US 10.5 (6.5 mm) or size needed to obtain gauge, US 10.5 (6.5 mm) set of 5 double-pointed needles or size needed to obtain gauge
- Stitch marker
- Scissors
- Yarn needle

GAUGE

S/M: Using US 10 (6 cm) needles, 15 sts x 19 rows in reverse stockinette = 4" (10 cm) square

L/XL: Using US 10.5 (6.5 cm) needles, 13 sts x 17 rows in reverse stockinette = 4" (10 cm) square

- Pattern instructions are the same throughout for both sizes; the only difference is the needle size.
- Hat is worked in rounds from bottom edge to crown. Switch from circular needles to double-pointed needles when necessary during crown shaping.
- Berroco Blackstone Tweed Chunky is a somewhat delicate fiber. Be careful to avoid excessive tugging at this yarn to minimize breakage.

Cast On

Using long-tail method and circular needle, CO 60 sts. Place a stitch marker between first and last sts and join in the round, being careful not to twist the cast-on row.

Brim

Rnd 1: Knit.
Rnd 2: Purl.
Rnd 3: Knit.
Rnd 4: Purl.
Rnd 5: Knit.

Body

Rnd 1: *P5, sl1k; rep from * around.
Rnd 2: *P5, k1; rep from * around.
Rnd 3: *P1, m1P, p4, sl1k; rep from * around—70 sts.
Rnd 4: *P6, k1; rep from * around.
Rnd 5: *P1, m1P, p5, sl1k; rep from * around—80 sts.
Rnd 6: *P7, k1; rep from * around.
Rnd 7: *P1, m1P, p6, sl1k; rep from * around—90 sts.
Rnd 8: *P8, k1; rep from * around.
Rnd 9: *P1, m1P, p7, sl1k; rep from * around—100 sts.
Even Rnds 10–22: *P9, k1; rep from * around.
Odd Rnds 11–21: *P9, sl1k; rep from * around.

Crown Shaping

Rnd 1: *P1, p2tog, p6, sl1k; rep from * around—90 sts.
Rnd 2: *P8, k1; rep from * around.
Rnd 3: *P1, p2tog, p5, sl1k; rep from * around—80 sts.
Rnd 4: *P7, k1; rep from * around.
Rnd 5: *P1, p2tog, p4, sl1k; rep from * around—70 sts.
Rnd 6: *P6, k1; rep from * around.
Rnd 7: *P1, p2tog, p3, sl1k; rep from * around—60 sts.
Rnd 8: *P5, k1; rep from * around.
Rnd 9: *P1, p2tog, p2, sl1k; rep from * around—50 sts.
Rnd 10: *P4, k1; rep from * around.
Rnd 11: *P1, p2tog, p1, sl1k; rep from * around—40 sts.
Rnd 12: *P3, k1; rep from * around.
Rnd 13: *P1, p2tog, sl1k; rep from * around—30 sts.
Rnd 14: *P2, k1; rep from * around.
Rnd 15: *P2tog, sl1k; rep from * around—20 sts.
Rnd 16: *P1, k1; rep from * around.
Rnd 17: *K2tog; rep from * around—10 sts.

Cut yarn, leaving an 8" (20.5 cm) tail. Thread yarn needle with end and pick up remaining stitches on knitting needles. Pull tightly to close and secure end. Weave in yarn tails on inside of hat.

Visor

These instructions are the same for either sized hat. Using long-tail method and 2 dpns (whichever size you used to knit the body of the hat), CO 7 sts.

Row 1: Knit.
Row 2: Purl.
Row 3: K3, m1L, k1, m1L, k3—9 sts.
Row 4: Purl.
Row 5: K3, m1L, k3, m1L, k3—11 sts.
Row 6: Purl.
Row 7: K3, m1L, k5, m1L, k3—13 sts.
Row 8: Purl.
Row 9: K3, m1L, k7, m1L, k3—15 sts.
Row 10: Purl.
Row 11: K3, m1L, k9, m1L, k3—17 sts.
Row 12: Purl.
Row 13: K3, m1L, k11, m1L, k3—19 sts.
Row 14: Purl.
Row 15: K3, m1L, k13, m1L, k3—21 sts.
Row 16: Purl.
Row 17: K3, m1L, k15, m1L, k3—23 sts.
Even Rows 18–26: Purl.
Odd Rows 19–25: Knit.
Row 27: K3, k2tog, k13, k2tog, k3—21 sts.
Row 28: Purl.
Row 29: K3, k2tog, k11, k2tog, k3—19 sts.
Row 30: Purl.
Row 31: K3, k2tog, k9, k2tog, k3—17 sts.
Row 32: Purl.
Row 33: K3, k2tog, k7, k2tog, k3—15 sts.
Row 34: Purl.
Row 35: K3, k2tog, k5, k2tog, k3—13 sts.
Row 36: Purl.
Row 37: K3, k2tog, k3, k2tog, k3—11 sts.
Row 38: Purl.
Row 39: K3, k2tog, k1, k2tog, k3—9 sts.
Row 40: Purl.
Row 41: K3, k2tog, k3—7 sts.
Row 42: Purl.

Finishing

BO and cut yarn, leaving 18" (46 cm) tail. Fold visor in half lengthwise, with wrong sides together. Use tail to sew edges together. Center folded edge of visor to bottom edge of hat brim and sew visor to brim. Flatten body of hat to overlap visor and sew a few stitches through visor and body of hat to secure.

Coaxial

Classic and handsome, this is the perfect pattern to learn basic cables. Use a smooth yarn with no fuzziness that might mask your crisp curves. An extra double-pointed needle can be substituted for a cable needle.

FINISHED MEASUREMENTS
Circumference at brim band 17" (43 cm) unstretched, 9" (23 cm) in length from brim edge to crown; will fit head circumference of 20" to 23" (50.5 to 58 cm)

YARN
125 yds (114 m) bulky weight #5 yarn (shown knitted in #M82 Blue Flannel, Brown Sheep Company Lamb's Pride Bulky, 85% wool, 15% mohair, 125 yds/114 m per skein)

NEEDLES AND OTHER MATERIALS
- One 16" (40.5 cm) circular knitting needle US 10.5 (6.5 mm) or size needed to obtain gauge
- US 10.5 (6.5 mm) set of 5 double-pointed needles or size needed to obtain gauge
- Stitch marker
- Cable needle
- Scissors
- Yarn needle

GAUGE
14 sts x 18 rows in stitch pattern = 4" (10 cm) square

SPECIAL STITCHES
2/2 Left Cross (2/2 LC): Slip next 2 sts to cable needle, hold cable needle to front of work, knit 2 sts from main needle, knit 2 sts from cable needle.

2/2 Left Cross Decrease (2/2 LC dec): Slip next 2 sts to cable needle, hold cable needle to front of work, knit 2 sts from main needle tog, knit 2 sts from cable needle.

STITCH PATTERN
Rnds 1–4: *K4, p2, k3, p2; rep from * around.
Rnd 5: *2/2 LC, p2, k3, p2; rep from * around.

Cast On

Using long-tail method and circular needle, CO 66 sts. Place a stitch marker between first and last sts and join in the round, being careful not to twist the cast-on row.

Brim and Body

Rnds 1–35: Work entire stitch patt 7 times.

Crown Shaping

Rnd 1: *K4, p2tog, k3, p2; rep from * around—60 sts.
Rnd 2: *K4, p1, k3, p2tog; rep from * around—54 sts.
Rnd 3: *K4, p1, k2tog, k1, p1; rep from * around—48 sts.
Rnd 4: *K4, p1, k2tog, p1; rep from * around—42 sts.
Rnd 5: *2/2 LC dec, p1, k1, p1; rep from * around—36 sts.
Rnd 6: *K2tog, k1, p1, k1, p1; rep from * around—30 sts.
Rnd 7: *K2tog, p1, k1, p1; rep from * around—24 sts.
Rnd 8: *K2tog; rep from * around—12 sts.

Finishing

Cut yarn, leaving an 8" (20.5 cm) tail. Thread yarn needle with end and pick up remaining stitches on knitting needles. Pull tightly to close and secure end. Weave in yarn tails on inside of hat.

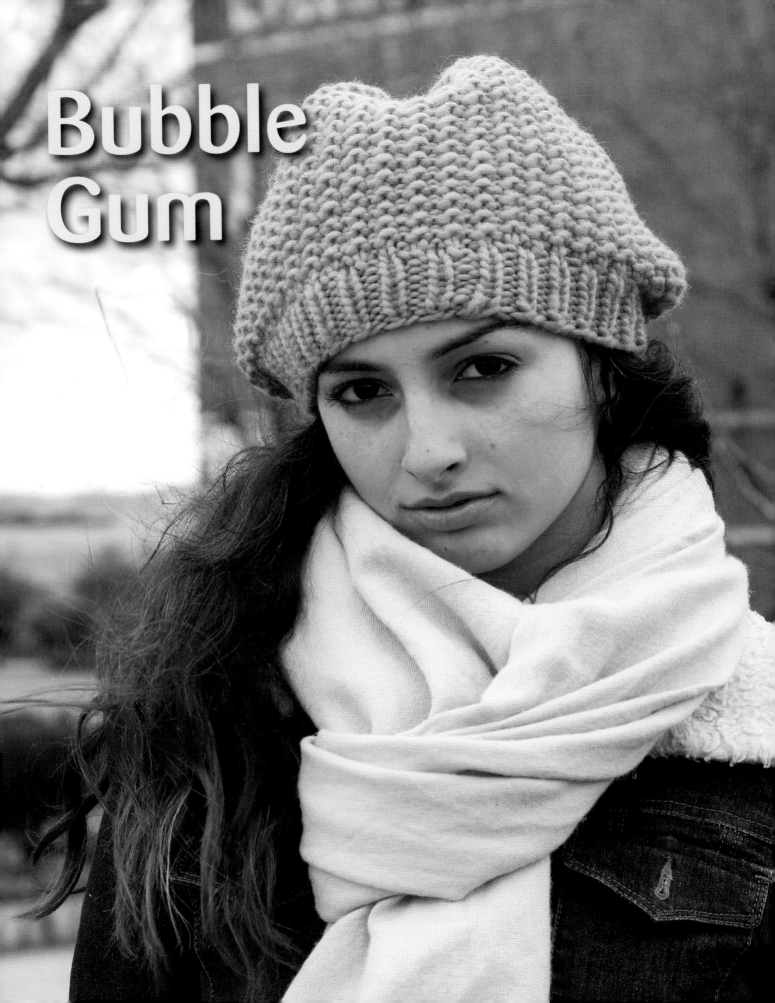

Bubble
Gum

ith a relaxing stitch pattern, this attractive hat knits up in no time. Use a chunky yarn with great stitch definition. The very best thing about this hat is that it is fully reversible!

FINISHED MEASUREMENTS
Circumference at brim band 19" (48 cm) unstretched, 9" (23 cm) in length from brim edge to crown; will fit head circumference of 20" to 23" (50.5 to 58 cm)

YARN
140 yds (128 m) bulky weight #5 yarn (shown knitted in #503 Vintage Rose, Martha Stewart Crafts Roving Wool, 100% wool, 58 yds/53 m per skein)

NEEDLES AND OTHER MATERIALS
- One 16" (40.5 cm) circular knitting needle US 10 (6 mm) or size needed to obtain gauge
- US 10 (6 mm) set of 5 double-pointed needles or size needed to obtain gauge
- Stitch marker
- Scissors
- Yarn needle

GAUGE
13 sts x 19 rows in stitch pattern = 4" (10 cm) square.

STITCH PATTERN
Rnd 1: *K1, p1; rep from * around.
Rnd 2: Purl.

Note

- Hat is worked in rounds from bottom edge to crown. Switch from circular needles to double-pointed needles when necessary during crown shaping.

Cast On

Using long-tail method and circular needle, CO 60 sts. Place a stitch marker between first and last sts and join in the round, being careful not to twist the cast-on row.

Brim

Rnds 1–8: *K1, p1; rep from * around.
Rnd 9: *K2, m1L; rep from * around—90 sts.

Body

Rnds 1–36: Work entire stitch pattern 18 times
Rnd 37: *K1, p1; rep from * around.

Crown

Rnd 1: *P3, sl1, p2tog, psso; rep from * around—60 sts.
Rnd 2: *K1, p1; rep from * around.
Rnd 3: *P1, sl1, p2tog, psso; rep from * around—30 sts.
Rnd 4: *K1, p1; rep from * around.
Rnd 5: *P2tog; rep from * around—15 sts.

Finishing

Cut yarn, leaving an 8" (20.5 cm) tail. Thread yarn needle with end and pick up remaining stitches on knitting needles. Pull tightly to close and secure end. Weave in yarn tails on inside of hat.

Urchin

The mushrooming volume of this deep slouch hat is created by building columns into wedges. These wedges are then strategically decreased every other round to create a crown of radial symmetry. The thick pleated stockinette ribbing is ideal for yarn with a slight fuzz or halo.

FINISHED MEASUREMENTS

S/M: Circumference at brim band 17" (43 cm) unstretched, 9" (23 cm) in length from brim edge to crown; will fit head circumference of 20" to 21" (50.5 to 53 cm)

L/XL: Circumference at brim band 18" (46 cm) unstretched, 10" (25 cm) in length from brim edge to crown; will fit head circumference of 22" to 23" (56 to 58 cm)

YARN

S/M: 180 yds (165 m) bulky weight #5 yarn (shown knitted in #M18 Khaki, Brown Sheep Company Lamb's Pride Bulky, 85% wool, 15% mohair, 125 yds/114 m per skein)

L/XL: 200 yds (183 m) bulky weight #5 yarn (shown knitted in #M02 Brown Heather, Brown Sheep Company Lamb's Pride Bulky, 85% wool, 15% mohair, 125 yds/114 m per skein)

NEEDLES AND OTHER MATERIALS

- **S/M:** One 16" (40.5 cm) circular knitting needle US 10 (6 mm) or size needed to obtain gauge, US 10 (6 mm) set of 5 double-pointed needles or size needed to obtain gauge
- **L/XL:** One 16" (40.5 cm) circular knitting needle US 10.5 (6.5 mm) or size needed to obtain gauge, US 10.5 (6.5 mm) set of 5 double-pointed needles or size needed to obtain gauge
- Stitch marker
- Scissors
- Yarn needle

GAUGE

S/M: Using US 10 (6 mm) needle, 14 sts x 18 rows in stockinette stitch = 4" (10 cm) square

L/XL: Using US 11 (6.5 mm) needle, 12 sts x 16 rows in stockinette stitch = 4" (10 cm) square

Knit in Brown Heather

Knit in Khaki

Cast On

Using long-tail method and circular needle, CO 64 sts. Place a stitch marker between first and last sts and join in the round, being careful not to twist the cast-on row.

Brim

Rnds 1–15: *K2, p2; rep from * around.

- Pattern instructions are the same throughout for both sizes; the only difference is the needle size.
- Hat is worked in rounds from bottom edge to crown. Switch from circular needles to double-pointed needles when necessary during crown shaping.

Body

Rnd 1: *Kfb, k1, p2; rep from * around—80 sts.
Rnd 2: *Kfb, k2, p2; rep from * around—96 sts.
Rnd 3: *Kfb, k3, p2; rep from * around—112 sts.
Rnd 4: *Kfb, k4, p2; rep from * around—128 sts.
Rnd 5: *Kfb, k5, p2; rep from * around—144 sts.
Rnds 6–15: *K7, p2; rep from * around.

Crown Shaping

Rnd 1: *K7, p2, k1, k2tog, k4, p2; rep from * around—136 sts.
Rnd 2: *K1, k2tog, k4, p2, k6, p2; rep from * around—128 sts.
Rnd 3: *K6, p2, k1, k2tog, k3, p2; rep from * around—120 sts.
Rnd 4: *K1, k2tog, k3, p2, k5, p2; rep from * around—112 sts.
Rnd 5: *K5, p2, k1, k2tog, k2, p2; rep from * around—104 sts.
Rnd 6: *K1, k2tog, k2, p2, k4, p2; rep from * around—96 sts.
Rnd 7: *K4, p2, k1, k2tog, k1, p2; rep from * around—88 sts.
Rnd 8: *K1, k2tog, k1, p2, k3, p2; rep from * around—80 sts.
Rnd 9: *K3, p2, k1, k2tog, p2; rep from * around—72 sts.
Rnd 10: *K1, k2tog, p2, k2, p2; rep from * around—64 sts.
Rnd 11: *K2, p2, k2tog, p2; rep from * around—56 sts.
Rnd 12: *K2tog, p2, k1, p2; rep from * around—48 sts.
Rnd 13: *K1, p2, k1, p2tog; rep from * around—40 sts.
Rnd 14: *K1, p2tog, k1, p1; rep from * around—32 sts.
Rnd 15: *K2tog; rep from * around—16 sts.

Finishing

Cut yarn, leaving an 8" (20.5 cm) tail. Thread yarn needle with end and pick up remaining stitches on knitting needles. Pull tightly to close and secure end. Weave in yarn tails on inside of hat.

Grape Jellyfish

This split-brim–style hat is adorned with a staggered bubble effect, created by a technique that might seem scary at first. As knitters, we all dread a dropped stitch, but in this project they are completely intentional. A smooth, solid yarn is best for this piece.

FINISHED MEASUREMENTS
Circumference at brim band 20" (50.5 cm), 9" (23 cm) in length from unrolled brim edge to crown; will fit head circumference of 20" to 23" (50.5 to 58 cm)

YARN
165 yds (151 m) bulky weight #5 yarn (shown knitted in #M162 Mulberry, Brown Sheep Company Lamb's Pride Bulky, 85% wool, 15% mohair, 125 yds/114 m per skein)

NEEDLES AND OTHER MATERIALS
- One 16" (40.5 cm) circular knitting needle US 11 (8 mm) or size needed to obtain gauge
- US 11 (8 mm) set of 5 double-pointed needles or size needed to obtain gauge
- Stitch marker
- Scissors
- Yarn needle

GAUGE
10 sts x 16 rows in stockinette st = 4" (10 cm) square

SPECIAL STITCH
Knit Stitch 5 Rows Below (k5b): Slip next stitch off the left needle and carefully let it drop 4 rows. Put right needle into front of dropped stitch and under the 4 loose strands. Knit stitch, gathering the 4 strands behind the stitch with it.

Cast On

Using long-tail method and circular needle, CO 100 sts. Do not join.

Brim

Row 1 (RS): K2tog, k to end—99 sts.
Row 2 (WS): P2tog, p to end—98 sts.
Row 3: K2tog, k to end—97 sts.
Row 4: P2tog, p to end—96 sts.
Row 5: K2tog, k to end—95 sts.
Row 6: P2tog, p to end—94 sts.
Row 7: K2tog, k to end—93 sts.
Row 8: P2tog, p to end—92 sts.
Row 9: K2tog, k to end—91 sts.
Row 10: P2tog, p to end—90 sts.
Row 11: BO 15 sts, k to end—75 sts.
Row 12: BO 15 sts, p to end—60 sts.
Row 13: Knit.
With the knit side facing out, join in the round. Place a stitch marker between first and last sts.
Rnds 1–3: Knit.
Rnd 4: *K3, m1L; rep from * around—80 sts.

Body

Rnds 1–5: Knit.
Rnd 6: *K5b, k3; rep from * around.
Rnds 7–11: Knit.
Rnd 12: K2, *k5b, k3; rep from * around until last 2 sts, k5b, k1.
Rnds 13–17: Knit.

Crown Shaping

Rnd 1: *K5b, k3; rep from * around.
Rnd 2: Knit.
Rnd 3: K5, k2tog, k2tog, *k4, k2tog, k2tog; rep from * around until last 7 sts, k4, k2tog, k1—61 sts.
Rnd 4: K5, k2tog, *k4, k2tog; rep from * around—51 sts.

Rnd 5: K4, k2tog, *k3, k2tog; rep from * around—41 sts.
Rnd 6: Knit.
Rnd 7: K2, *k5b, k3; rep from * around until last 3 sts, k5b, k2.
Rnds 8–9: Knit.
Rnd 10: *K3, k2tog; rep from * around until last st, k1—33 sts.
Rnd 11: Knit.
Rnd 12: *K1, k2tog; rep from * around—22 sts.
Rnd 13: *K2tog; rep from * around—11 sts.

Finishing

Cut yarn leaving an 8" (20.5 cm) tail. Thread yarn needle with end and pick up remaining stitches on knitting needles. Pull tightly to close and secure end. Weave in yarn tails on inside of hat.
Make two 2" (5 cm) pom-poms. Feed the tail ends through the elongated brim ties and secure. Trim ends.

Kaleidoscope

As eye-catching as it is easy, this riot of color looks to be knit from many different yarns when it really is only one solid-color and one self-striping yarn. Begin the brim with a corrugated rib pattern, then follow the charts provided.

FINISHED MEASUREMENTS

Circumference at brim band 18" (46 cm) unstretched, 8.5" (22 cm) in length from brim edge to crown; will fit head circumference of 20" to 23" (50.5 to 58 cm)

YARN

Color A: 100 yds (91 m) bulky weight #5 yarn (shown knitted in #M005 Onyx, Brown Sheep Lamb's Pride Bulky, 85% wool, 15% mohair, 125 yds/114 m per skein)

Color B: 100 yds (91 m) bulky weight #5 yarn (shown knitted in #661 Wicked, King Cole Riot Chunky, 70% acrylic, 30% wool, 147 yds/134 m per skein)

NEEDLES AND OTHER MATERIALS

- One 16" (40.5 cm) circular knitting needle US 10.5 (6.5 mm) or size needed to obtain gauge
- US 10.5 (6.5 mm) set of 5 double-pointed needles or size needed to obtain gauge
- Stitch marker
- Scissors
- Yarn needle

GAUGE

14 sts x 18 rows in stockinette stitch = 4" (10 cm) square

- Hat is worked in rounds from bottom edge to crown. Switch from circular needle to double-pointed needles when necessary during crown shaping.
- In the directions for the Stitch Pattern and the Crown Shaping, A and B refer to the yarn colors.
- Color charts are read from bottom to top and from right to left.
- Knitting a pattern in two colors is called stranding. Only one color is knit at a time, while the other color will wait its turn and be carried behind the work until it is used again. Be certain that the carried yarn remains at a relaxed tension. When switching from one color to the other, Color A should always strand from underneath Color B and Color B should always be carried above Color A.
- For a photo tutorial on how to make pom-poms, see page 133.

STITCH PATTERN

Rnd 1: *k6A, k6B; rep from * around.
Rnd 2: *K1B, k5A, k5B, k1A; rep from * around.
Rnd 3: *K2B, k4A, k4B, k2A; rep from * around.
Rnd 4: *K3B, k3A, k3B, k3A; rep from * around.
Rnd 5: *K4B, k2A, k2B, k4A; rep from * around.
Rnd 6: *K5B, k1A, k1B, k5A; rep from * around.
Rnd 7: *K6B, k6A; rep from * around.
Rnd 8: *K6A, k6B; rep from * around.
Rnd 9: *K5A, k1B, k1A, k5B; rep from * around.
Rnd 10: *K4A, k2B, k2A, k4B; rep from * around.
Rnd 11: *K3A, k3B, k3A, k3B; rep from * around.
Rnd 12: *K2A, k4B, k4A, k2B; rep from * around.
Rnd 13: *K1A, k5B, k5A, k1B; rep from * around.
Rnd 14: *K6B, k6A; rep from * around.

Cast On

Using long-tail method, Color A, and circular needle, CO 60 sts. Place a stitch marker between first and last sts and join in the round, being careful not to twist the cast-on row.

Brim

Rnds 1–8: *K1A, p1B; rep from * around.
Rnd 9: *k2, m1L, k3, m1L; rep from * around—84 sts.

Body

Rnds 1–35: In stockinette stitch, work entire stitch pattern 2 times, then work rnds 1-7 of stitch patt one time.

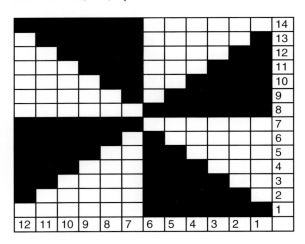

■ Color A
□ Color B

Stitch Pattern

Crown Shaping

Rnd 1: *K6A, k6B*; rep from * around.

Rnd 2: *SskA, k3A, k1B, k1A, k3B, k2togB; rep from * around—70 sts.

Rnd 3: *K3A, k2B, k2A, k3B; rep from * around.

Rnd 4: *K2A, k1B, k2togB, sskA, k1A, k2B; rep from * around—56 sts.

Rnd 5: *K1A, k3B, k3A, k1B; rep from * around.

Rnd 6: *K2togB, k2B, sskA, k2A; rep from * around—42 sts.

Rnd 7: *K3A, k3B; rep from * around.

Rnd 8: *K2togA, k1A, k2togB, k1B; rep from * around—28 sts.

Rnd 9: *K2togA, k2togB; rep from * around—14 sts.

Rnd 10: *K2togA; rep from * around—7 sts.

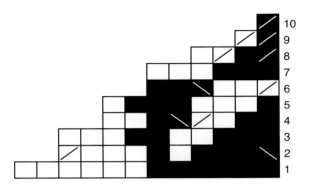

- ■ Color A Knit
- ◪ Color A K2tog
- ◪ Color A SSK

- □ Color B Knit
- ◩ Color B K2tog
- ◪ Color B SSK

Stitch Pattern
for Crown Shaping

Finishing

Cut yarns, leaving 8" (20.5 cm) tails. Thread yarn needle with Color A end and pick up remaining stitches on knitting needles. Pull tightly to close and secure both yarn ends. Weave in yarn tails on inside of hat.

Smocking
Stocking
Cap

The technique of smocking gathers stitches together and creates a richly textured stretchy fabric, perfect for the brim band of a hat. A stocking cap, sometimes also called a toboggan cap, is a long, narrowing hat with a tassel at the end that catches the wind as your sled races downhill. The combination of stockinette and smocking really shows off the complexities of a hand-dyed yarn.

FINISHED MEASUREMENTS
Circumference at brim band 16" (41 cm) unstretched, 17" (43 cm) in length from brim edge to crown tip; will fit head circumference of 20" to 23" (50.5 to 58 cm)

YARN
280 yds (256 m) heavy worsted weight #4 yarn (shown knitted in #51 VAA, Malabrigo Worsted Merino, 100% merino wool, 210 yds/192 m per skein)

NEEDLES AND OTHER MATERIALS
- One 16" (40.5 cm) circular knitting needle US 7 (4.5 mm) or size needed to obtain gauge
- One US 7 (4.5 mm) set of 5 double-pointed needles or size needed to obtain gauge
- Stitch marker
- Scissors
- Yarn needle

GAUGE
20 sts x 24 rows in stockinette st = 4" (10 cm) square

SPECIAL STITCH
Smocking Stitch (Smkst): Insert right needle between stitches 6 and 7 on left needle, pull a loop of working yarn through, and place it on the end of the left needle. Knit this new loop together with the first stitch.

Note

- Hat is worked in rounds from bottom edge to crown. Switch from circular needles to double-pointed needles when necessary during crown shaping.
- For photo tutorials on smocking stitch and how to make a tassel, see pages 122 and 134.

Cast On

Using long-tail method and circular needle, CO 104 sts. Place a stitch marker between first and last sts and join in the round, being careful not to twist the cast-on row.

Brim

Rnds 1–3: *K2, p2; rep from * around.
Rnd 4: *Smkst, k1, p2, k2, p2; rep from * around.
Rnds 5–6: *K2, p2; rep from * around.
Rnd 7: *K2, p2; rep from * around until the last 4 sts. Slip 4 to right hand needle, remove stitch marker, replace 4 slipped sts to left hand needle, replace marker.
Rnd 8: *Smkst, k1, p2, k2, p2; rep from * around.
Rnd 9: Remove stitch marker, k2, p2, replace stitch marker, *k2, p2; rep from * around.
Rnds 10–11: *K2, p2; rep from * around.
Rnd 12: *Smkst, k1, p2, k2, p2; rep from * around.
Rnds 13–14: *K2, p2; rep from * around.
Rnd 15: *K2, p2; rep from * around until the last 4 sts. Slip 4 to right hand needle, remove stitch marker, replace 4 slipped sts to left hand needle, replace marker.
Rnd 16: *Smkst, k1, p2, k2, p2; rep from * around.
Rnd 17: Remove stitch marker, k2, p2, replace stitch marker, *k2, p2; rep from * around.
Rnds 18–19: *K2, p2; rep from * around.

Body

Rnds 1–23: Knit.

Crown Shaping

Rnd 1: *K24, k2tog; rep from * around—100 sts.
Rnds 2–5: Knit.
Rnd 6: *K23, k2tog; rep from * around—96 sts.
Rnds 7–10: Knit.
Rnd 11: *K22, k2tog; rep from * around—92 sts.
Rnds 12–15: Knit.
Rnd 16: *K21, k2tog; rep from * around—88 sts.
Rnds 17–20: Knit.
Rnd 21: *K20, k2tog; rep from * around—84 sts.
Rnds 22–25: Knit.
Rnd 26: *K19, k2tog; rep from * around—80 sts.
Rnds 27–30: Knit.
Rnd 31: *K18, k2tog; rep from * around—76 sts.
Rnds 32–34: Knit.
Rnd 35: *K17, k2tog; rep from * around—72 sts.
Rnds 36–38: Knit.
Rnd 39: *K16, k2tog; rep from * around—68 sts.
Rnds 40–42: Knit.
Rnd 43: *K15, k2tog; rep from * around—64 sts.
Rnds 44–46: Knit.
Rnd 47: *K14, k2tog; rep from * around—60 sts.
Rnds 48–50: Knit.
Rnd 51: *K13, k2tog; rep from * around—56 sts.
Rnds 52–54: Knit.
Rnd 55: *K12, k2tog; rep from * around—52 sts.
Rnds 56–58: Knit.
Rnd 59: *K11, k2tog; rep from * around—48 sts.
Rnds 60–61: Knit.
Rnd 62: *K10, k2tog; rep from * around—44 sts.
Rnds 63–64: Knit.
Rnd 65: *K9, k2tog; rep from * around—40 sts.
Rnds 66–67: Knit.
Rnd 68: *K8, k2tog; rep from * around—36 sts.
Rnds 69–70: Knit.
Rnd 71: *K7, k2tog; rep from * around—32 sts.
Rnds 72–73: Knit.
Rnd 74: *K6, k2tog; rep from * around—28 sts.
Rnds 75–76: Knit.
Rnd 77: *K5, k2tog; rep from * around—24 sts.
Rnds 78–79: Knit.
Rnd 80: *K4, k2tog; rep from * around—20 sts.
Rnd 81: Knit.
Rnd 82: *K3, k2tog; rep from * around—16 sts.
Rnd 83: Knit
Rnd 84: *K2, k2tog; rep from * around—12 sts.
Rnd 85: Knit.
Rnd 86: *K1, k2tog; rep from * around—8 sts.

Finishing

Cut yarn, leaving an 8" (20.5 cm) tail. Thread yarn needle with end and pick up remaining stitches on knitting needles. Pull tightly to close and secure end. Weave in all yarn tails on inside of hat.

Make a 6" (15 cm) tassel. Feed the top knot tails of the tassel through the tip of the hat and secure, then use the yarn needle to feed those ends down through the tassel. Trim ends as needed.

Ribs
& Twists

In this contemporary hat pattern, unconventional ribbing travels from brim to crown, framing lacework panels that resemble twisted stitches. With its open weave, this hat is a great transitional piece for spring or fall. It can easily be made slouchy just by continuing the body rounds until you reach your desired length.

FINISHED MEASUREMENTS

Circumference at brim band 17" (43 cm) unstretched, 8" (20 cm) in length from brim edge to crown; will fit head circumference of 20" to 23" (50.5 to 58 cm)

YARN

175 yds (160 m) worsted weight #4 yarn (shown knitted in #M81 Red Baron, Brown Sheep Company Lamb's Pride Worsted, 85% wool, 15% mohair, 190 yds/173 m per skein)

NEEDLES AND OTHER MATERIALS

- One 16" (40.5 cm) circular knitting needle US 7 (4.5 mm) or size needed to obtain gauge
- US 7 (4.5 mm) set of 5 double-pointed needles or size needed to obtain gauge
- Stitch marker
- Scissors
- Yarn needle

GAUGE

20 sts x 24 rows in stitch pattern = 4" (10 cm) square

STITCH PATTERN

Rnd 1: Knit.
Rnd 2: *K1, p1, k1, yo, sl1, k2tog, psso, yo; rep from * around.

- Hat is worked in rounds from bottom edge to crown. Switch from circular needles to double-pointed needles when necessary during crown shaping.

Cast On

Using long-tail method and circular needle, CO 90 sts. Place a stitch marker between first and last sts and join in the round, being careful not to twist the cast-on row.

Brim

Rnd 1: *K3, p3; rep from * around.
Rnd 2: *K1, p1, k1, p3; rep from * around.
Repeat rnds 1 and 2 three more times, for a total of 8 rnds.

Body

Rnds 1–40: Work entire stitch pattern 20 times.

Crown Shaping

Rnd 1: Knit.
Rnd 2: *K1, p1, k1, sl1, k2tog, psso; rep from * around—60 sts.
Rnd 3: Knit.
Rnd 4: *K2tog; rep from * around—30 sts.
Rnd 5: Knit.
Rnd 6: *K2tog; rep from * around—15 sts.

Finishing

Cut yarn, leaving an 8" (20.5 cm) tail. Thread yarn needle with end and pick up remaining stitches on knitting needles. Pull tightly to close and secure end. Weave in yarn tails on inside of hat.

Vermont
Foliage

This lacy pattern, knit in a bold autumn tweed, evokes an image of freshly raked piles of leaves. Jump in! Grab a cup of hot cider, curl up in your favorite chair, and watch your new favorite hat come together in a cascade of delicate stitch work.

FINISHED MEASUREMENTS

Circumference at brim band 16" (41 cm) unstretched, 8" (20 cm) in length from brim edge to crown; will fit head circumference of 20" to 23" (50.5 to 58 cm)

YARN

200 yds (183 m) worsted weight #4 yarn (shown knitted in #84605 Paprika Tweed, Patons Classic Wool Merino Tweeds, 90% wool, 7% acrylic, 3% viscose, 223 yds/205 m per skein)

NEEDLES AND OTHER MATERIALS

- One 16" (40.5 cm) circular knitting needle US 6 (4 mm) or size needed to obtain gauge
- US 6 (4 mm) set of 5 double-pointed needles or size needed to obtain gauge
- Stitch marker
- Scissors
- Yarn needle

GAUGE

22 sts x 28 rows in stitch pattern = 4" (10 cm) square

Note

- Hat is worked in rounds from bottom edge to crown. Switch from circular needles to double-pointed needles when necessary during crown shaping.
- See page 72 for foliage stitch pattern charts for the Body and Crown Shaping.

Cast On

Using long-tail method and circular needle, CO 96 sts. Place a stitch marker between first and last sts and join in the round, being careful not to twist the cast-on row.

Brim

Rnds 1–10: *K1, p1; rep from * around.
Rnd 11: *K6, m1L; rep from * around—112 sts.

Body

Rnd 1: *K11, p2, k1, p2; rep from * around.
Rnd 2: *Ssk, k7, k2tog, p2, yo, k1tbl, yo, p2; rep from * around.
Rnd 3: *K9, p2, k1, k1tbl, k1, p2; rep from * around.
Rnd 4: *Ssk, k5, k2tog, p2, k1, yo, k1tbl, yo, k1, p2; rep from * around.
Rnd 5: *K7, p2, k2, k1tbl, k2, p2; rep from * around.
Rnd 6: *Ssk, k3, k2tog, p2, k2, yo, k1tbl, yo, k2, p2; rep from * around.
Rnd 7: *K5, p2, k3, k1tbl, k3, p2; rep from * around.
Rnd 8: *Ssk, k1, k2tog, p2, k3, yo, k1tbl, yo, k3, p2; rep from * around.
Rnd 9: *K3, p2, k4, k1tbl, k4, p2; rep from * around.
Rnd 10: *Sl1, k2tog, psso, p2, k4, yo, k1, yo, k4, p2; rep from * around.
Rnd 11: *K1, p2, k11, p2; rep from * around.
Rnd 12: *Yo, k1tbl, yo, p2, ssk, k7, k2tog, p2; rep from * around.
Rnd 13: *K1, k1tbl, k1, p2, k9, p2; rep from * around.
Rnd 14: *K1, yo, k1tbl, yo, k1, p2, ssk, k5, k2tog, p2; rep from * around.
Rnd 15: *K2, k1tbl, k2, p2, k7, p2; rep from * around.
Rnd 16: *K2, yo, k1tbl, yo, k2, p2, ssk, k3, k2tog, p2; rep from * around.
Rnd 17: *K3, k1tbl, k3, p2, k5, p2; rep from * around.
Rnd 18: *K3, yo, k1tbl, yo, k3, p2, ssk, k1, k2tog, p2; rep from * around.
Rnd 19: *K4, k1tbl, k4, p2, k3, p2; rep from * around.
Rnd 20: *K4, yo, k1, yo, k4, p2, sl1, k2tog, psso, p2; rep from * around.

Repeat body Rounds 1–20 once more, then move on to the crown shaping.

Crown Shaping

Rnd 1: *K11, p2, k1, p2; rep from * around.
Rnd 2: *Ssk, k7, k2tog, p2, k1, p2; rep from * around—98 sts.
Rnd 3: *K9, p2, k1, p2; rep from * around.
Rnd 4: *Ssk, k5, k2tog, p2, k1, p2; rep from * around—84 sts.
Rnd 5: *K7, p5; rep from * around.
Rnd 6: *Ssk, k3, k2tog, p2, k1, p2; rep from * around—70 sts.
Rnd 7: *K5, p5; rep from * around.
Rnd 8: *Ssk, k1, k2tog, p2, k1, p2; rep from * around—56 sts.
Rnd 9: *K3, p5; rep from * around.
Rnd 10: *Sl1, k2tog, psso, p2, k1, p2; rep from * around—42 sts.
Rnd 11: *K1, p2tog, k1, p2tog; rep from * around—28 sts.
Rnd 12: *K2tog; rep from * around—14 sts.

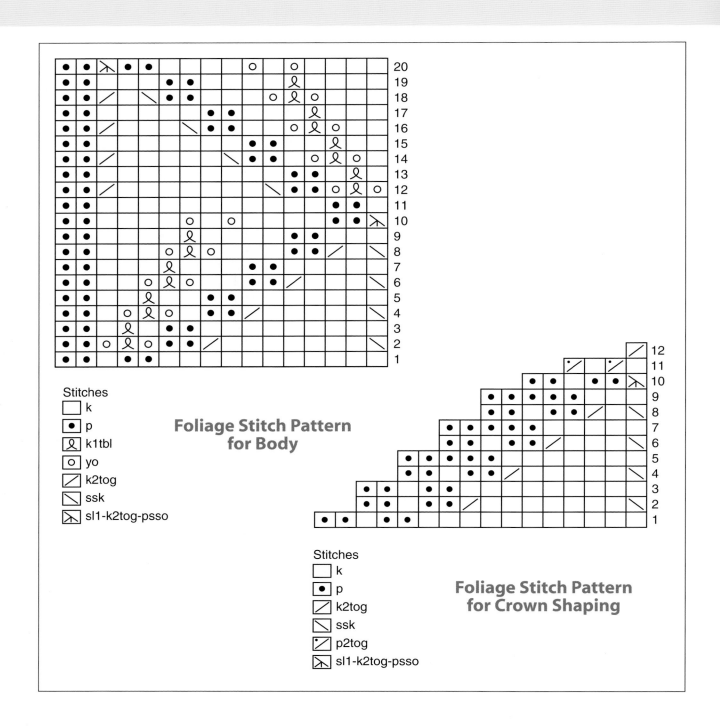

Foliage Stitch Pattern for Body

Stitches

- ☐ k
- ⊡ p
- 𝕏 k1tbl
- ○ yo
- ⧄ k2tog
- ⧅ ssk
- ⋈ sl1-k2tog-psso

Foliage Stitch Pattern for Crown Shaping

Stitches

- ☐ k
- ⊡ p
- ⧄ k2tog
- ⧅ ssk
- ⧄ p2tog
- ⋈ sl1-k2tog-psso

Finishing

Cut yarn, leaving an 8" (20.5 cm) tail. Thread yarn needle
with end and pick up remaining stitches on knitting
needles. Pull tightly to close and secure end. Weave in
yarn tails on inside of hat.

Native
American
Geometric

Inspired by ancient textiles, this diamond and chevron pattern is based on Native American geometric imagery. Reflect on the warmth of the desert with these bold traditional earthen colors. Dimpling in the end corners of the triangular-shaped crown seams adds depth and interest.

FINISHED MEASUREMENTS
Circumference at brim band 20" (51 cm) unstretched, 9" (23 cm) in length from brim edge to crown; will fit head circumference of 20" to 23" (50.5 to 58 cm)

YARN
Color A: 100 yds (91 m) worsted weight #4 yarn (shown knitted in Spice, Valley Yarns Amherst, 100% merino wool, 109 yds/100 m per skein)

Color B: 50 yds (46 m) worsted weight #4 yarn (shown knitted in Natural, Valley Yarns Amherst, 100% merino wool, 109 yds/100 m per skein)

Color C: 50 yds (46 m) worsted weight #4 yarn (shown knitted in Chocolate, Valley Yarns Amherst, 100% merino wool, 109 yds/100 m per skein)

NEEDLES AND OTHER MATERIALS
- One 16" (40.5 cm) circular knitting needle US 7 (4.5 mm) or size needed to obtain gauge
- One US 7 (4.5 mm) double-pointed needle or size needed to obtain gauge
- Stitch marker
- Scissors
- Yarn needle

GAUGE
24 sts x 24 rows in stockinette stitch = 4" (10 cm) square

Note

- Hat is worked in rounds from bottom edge to crown. Switch from circular needles to double-pointed needles when necessary during crown shaping.
- Color charts are read from bottom to top and from right to left.
- Knitting a pattern in multiple colors is called stranding. Only one color is knit at a time, while the other colors will wait their turn and be carried behind the work until they are used again. Be certain that the carried yarns remain at a relaxed tension. To keep the inside of your work tidy when switching from one color to another, be consistent regarding which color strands are carried underneath or above the previous color. When working sections that do not include one of the colors, run this unworked color up the side of the work by twisting it with the main color used at the end of the round rather than cutting it and reattaching it each time it is needed.

Cast On

Using long-tail method and circular needle, CO 90 sts in Color A. Place a stitch marker between first and last sts and join in the round, being careful not to twist the cast-on row.

Brim

Rnds 1–8: *K1, p1; rep from * around.
Rnd 9: *K3, m1L; rep from * around—120 sts.

Body

Rnds 1–35: Working in stockinette stitch, follow the entire Body Color Chart for 35 rnds.

Crown Shaping

Continue in Color A.
Rnd 1: *Ssk, k26, k2tog; rep from * around—112 sts.
Rnd 2: *Ssk, k24, k2tog; rep from * around—104 sts.
Rnd 3: *Ssk, k22, k2tog; rep from * around—96 sts.
Rnd 4: *Ssk, k20, k2tog; rep from * around—88 sts.
Rnd 5: *Ssk, k18, k2tog; rep from * around—80 sts.
Rnd 6: *Ssk, k16, k2tog; rep from * around—72 sts.
Rnd 7: *Ssk, k14, k2tog; rep from * around—64 sts.
Rnd 8: *Ssk, k12, k2tog; rep from * around—56 sts.
Rnd 9: *Ssk, k10, k2tog; rep from * around—48 sts.
Rnd 10: *Ssk, k8, k2tog; rep from * around—40 sts.
Rnd 11: *Ssk, k6, k2tog; rep from * around—32 sts.
Rnd 12: *Ssk, k4, k2tog; rep from * around—24 sts.
Rnd 13: *Ssk, k2, k2tog; rep from * around—16 sts.
Rnd 14: *Ssk, k2tog; rep from * around—8 sts.

Finishing

Cut yarn, leaving an 8" (20.5 cm) tail. Thread yarn needle with end and pick up remaining stitches on knitting needles. Pull tightly to close and secure end. Weave in yarn tails on inside of hat.

Color A

Color B

Color C

Body Color Chart

Jubilee

Queen Elizabeth II's Diamond Jubilee was the inspiration behind this knit. Strong, yet subtle, with a gentle drape, this slouchy hat features a slight rolled edge detail and a double-diamond brocade pattern. Choose a plain DK weight yarn that will show off all of your beautiful stitch work.

FINISHED MEASUREMENTS

Circumference at brim band 19" (48 cm) unstretched, 9" (23 cm) in length from brim edge to crown; will fit head circumference of 20" to 23" (50.5 to 58 cm)

YARN

220 yds (201 m) DK weight #4 yarn (shown knitted in #0033 Slate, Willow Yarns Daily DK, 100% superwash wool, 284 yds/260 m per skein)

NEEDLES AND OTHER MATERIALS

- One 16" (40.5 cm) circular knitting needle US 5 (3.75 mm) or size needed to obtain gauge
- US 5 (3.75 mm) set of 5 double-pointed needles or size needed to obtain gauge
- Stitch marker
- Scissors
- Yarn needle

GAUGE

22 sts x 28 rows in stitch pattern = 4" (10 cm) square

STITCH PATTERN

Rnd 1: *K9, p1, k1, p1; rep from * around.
Rnd 2: *P1, k7, p1, k1, p1, k1; rep from * around.
Rnd 3: *K1, p1, k5, p1, k1, p1, k1, p1; rep from * around.
Rnd 4: *P1, k1, p1, k3; rep from * around.
Rnd 5: K1, *p1, k1, p1, k1, p1, k1, p1, k5 *; repeat from * to * until last 11 sts, p1, k1, p1, k1, p1, k1, p1, k4.
Rnd 6: K2, *p1, k1, p1, k1, p1, k7 *; repeat from * to * until last 10 sts, p1, k1, p1, k1, p1, k5.
Rnd 7: K3, *p1, k1, p1, k9 *; repeat from * to * until last 9 sts, p1, k1, p1, k6.

Note

- Hat is worked in rounds from bottom edge to crown. Switch from circular needles to double-pointed needles when necessary during crown shaping.

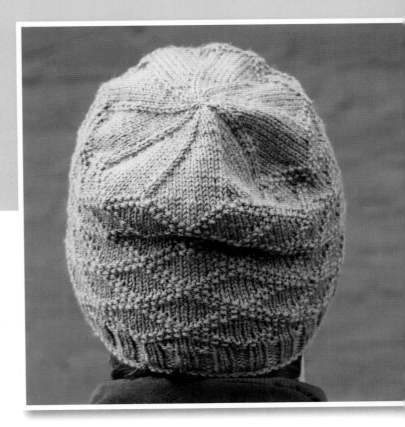

Rnd 8: K2, *p1, k1, p1, k1, p1, k7 *; repeat from * to * until last 10 sts, p1, k1, p1, k1, p1, k5.

Rnd 9: K1, *p1, k1, p1, k1, p1, k1, p1, k5 *; repeat from * to * until last 11 sts, p1, k1, p1, k1, p1, k1, p1, k4.

Rnd 10: *P1, k1, p1, k3; rep from * around.

Rnd 11: *K1, p1, k5, p1, k1, p1, k1, p1; rep from * around.

Rnd 12: *P1, k7, p1, k1, p1, k1; rep from * around.

Cast On

Using long-tail method and circular needle, CO 108 sts. Place a stitch marker between first and last sts and join in the round, being careful not to twist the cast-on row.

Brim

Rnds 1–3: Knit.
Rnds 4–12: *K2, p2; rep from * around.

Body

Rnds 1–48: Work entire stitch patt 4 times.

Crown Shaping

Rnd 1: *K9, p1, k1, p1; rep from * around.
Rnd 2: Knit.
Rnd 3: *K10, k2tog; rep from * around—99 sts.
Rnd 4: Knit.
Rnd 5: *K9, k2tog; rep from * around—90 sts.
Rnd 6: Knit.
Rnd 7: *K8, k2tog; rep from * around—81 sts.
Rnd 8: Knit.
Rnd 9: *K7, k2tog; rep from * around—72 sts.
Rnd 10: Knit.
Rnd 11: *K6, k2tog; rep from * around—63 sts.
Rnd 12: Knit.
Rnd 13: *K5, k2tog; rep from * around—54 sts.
Rnd 14: Knit.
Rnd 15: *K4, k2tog; rep from * around—45 sts.

Rnd 16: Knit.
Rnd 17: *K3, k2tog; rep from * around—36 sts.
Rnd 18: Knit.
Rnd 19: *K2, k2tog; rep from * around—27 sts.
Rnd 20: Knit.
Rnd 21: *K1, k2tog; rep from * around—18 sts.
Rnd 22: Knit.
Rnd 23: *K2tog; rep from * around—9 sts.

Finishing

Cut yarn, leaving an 8" (20.5 cm) tail. Thread yarn needle with end and pick up remaining stitches on knitting needles. Pull tightly to close and secure end. Weave in yarn tails on inside of hat.

Twofer

uch like watching snowflakes collect on a windowsill, Fair Isle knitting begins as dashes and dots that soon build into beautifully woven color patterns. Every new round is as exciting as the last. A simple eyelet channel encases a handmade cord, and with a pull of the cord this clever knit transforms from cowl into cozy hat.

FINISHED MEASUREMENTS

Circumference at brim band 23" (58 m) unstretched, 11.5 inches (29 m) from brim band to top edge; will fit head circumference of 20" to 23" (50.5 to 58 cm).

YARN

Color A: 120 yds (110 m) worsted weight #4 yarn (shown knitted in #191 Violet, Lion Brand Yarn Wool-Ease Worsted Weight, 80% acrylic, 20% wool, 197 yds/180 m per skein)

Color B: 70 yds (64 m) worsted weight #4 yarn (shown knitted in #177 Loden, Lion Brand Yarn Wool-Ease Worsted Weight, 80% acrylic, 20% wool, 197 yds/180 m per skein)

Color C: 70 yds (64 m) worsted weight #4 yarn (shown knitted in #123 Seaspray, Lion Brand Yarn Wool-Ease Worsted Weight, 80% acrylic, 20% wool, 197 yds/180 m per skein)

Color D: 70 yds (64 m) worsted weight #4 yarn (shown knitted in #184 Aloe, Lion Brand Yarn Wool-Ease Worsted Weight, 80% acrylic, 20% wool, 197 yds/180 m per skein)

NEEDLES AND OTHER MATERIALS

- One 16" (40.5 cm) circular knitting needle US 8 (5 mm) or size needed to obtain gauge
- Stitch marker
- Scissors
- Yarn needle

GAUGE

18 sts x 24 rows in stockinette stitch = 4" (10 cm) square

Note

- Hat is worked in rounds from bottom edge to top.
- Color charts are read from bottom to top and from right to left.
- Knitting a pattern in multiple colors is called stranding. Only one color is knit at a time, while the other colors will wait their turn and be carried behind the work until they are used again. Be certain that the carried yarns remain at a relaxed tension. To keep the inside of your work tidy when switching from one color to another, be consistent regarding which color strands are carried underneath or above the previous color. When working sections that do not include one of the colors, run this unworked color up the side of the work by twisting it with the main color used at the end of the round rather than cutting it and reattaching it each time it is needed.
- For a photo tutorial on making a twisted cord, see page 135.

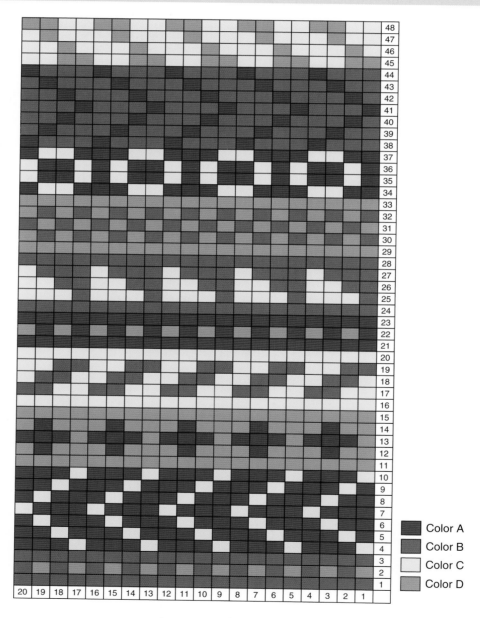

Body Color Chart

Cast On

Using long-tail method and circular needle, CO 90 sts in Color A. Place a stitch marker between first and last sts and join in the round, being careful not to twist the cast-on row.

Brim

Rnd 1: *P1, sl1p; rep from * around.
Rnd 2: *K1, P1; rep from * around.
Rnds 3–4: Knit.
Rnds 5–8: Rep Rnds 1–4.
Rnds 9–10: Rep Rnds 1–2.
Rnd 11: Knit.
Rnd 12: *K3, m1L; rep from * around—120 sts.

Body

Rnds 1–48: Working in stockinette stitch, follow the entire Body Color Chart for 48 rnds.
Continue in Color A.
Rnds 49–50: Knit.
Rnd 51: *K4, yo, k2tog; rep from * around.
Rnds 52–53: Knit.
Rnd 54: *K1, p1; rep from * around.
Rnd 55: *P1, sl1p; rep from * around.
Rnds 56–57: Knit.
Rnd 58: *K1, p1; rep from * around.
Rnd 59: *P1, sl1p; rep from * around.
Rnd 60: Knit.

Finishing

BO loosely. Secure end and weave in yarn tails on inside of hat.
Make a 5' (1.5 m) twisted cord, starting with 240" lengths of both colors C and D. Weave this cord in and out of the yarn-over eyelets created in rnd 51 at the top of the cowl. Wear opened and loose for a cowl, or pull both ends of the cord to gather and secure with a bow to transform into a hat.

Variation

Rhubarb

Show off a fabulous yarn with this quick ribbed knit. Casting on with the smaller needles allows for a tighter brim. Progressing to larger needles makes for a lofty crown.

FINISHED MEASUREMENTS

Circumference at brim band 17" (43 cm) unstretched, 11.5" (29 cm) in length from brim edge to crown; will fit head circumference of 20" to 23" (50.5 to 58 cm)

YARN

140 yds (128 m) bulky weight #5 yarn (shown knitted in 513 Winterberry, Martha Stewart Crafts Alpaca Blend, 40% wool, 40% acrylic, 20% alpaca, 115 yds/105 m per skein)

NEEDLES AND OTHER MATERIALS

- One 16" (40.5 cm) circular knitting needle US 10 (6 mm) or size needed to obtain gauge
- One 16" (40.5 cm) circular knitting needle US 11 (8 mm) or size needed to obtain gauge
- US 11 (8 mm) set of 5 double-pointed needles or size needed to obtain gauge
- Stitch marker
- Scissors
- Yarn needle

GAUGE

With US 10 (6 mm) needles, 13 sts x 18 rows in rib pattern = 4" (10 cm) square

Cast On

Using long-tail method and size US 10 (6 mm) circular needle, CO 72 sts. Place a stitch marker between first and last sts and join in the round, being careful not to twist the cast-on row.

Brim

Rnds 1–12: *K1, p1; rep from * around.

Body

Switch to size US 11 (8 mm) circular needle.
Rnds 1–28: *K1, p1; rep from * around.

Crown Shaping

Rnd 1: *K1, p1, k1, p1, k1, sl1, k2tog, psso; rep from * around—54 sts.
Rnd 2: *K1, p1; rep from * around.
Rnd 3: *K1, p1, k1, sl1, k2tog, psso; rep from * around—36 sts.
Rnd 4: *K1, p1; rep from * around.
Rnd 5: *K1, sl1, k2tog, psso; rep from * around—18 sts.
Rnd 6: *K1, p1; rep from * around.
Rnd 7: *K2tog; rep from * around—9 sts.

Finishing

Cut yarn, leaving an 8" (20.5 cm) tail. Thread yarn needle with end and pick up remaining stitches on knitting needles. Pull tightly to close and secure end. Weave in yarn tails on inside of hat.

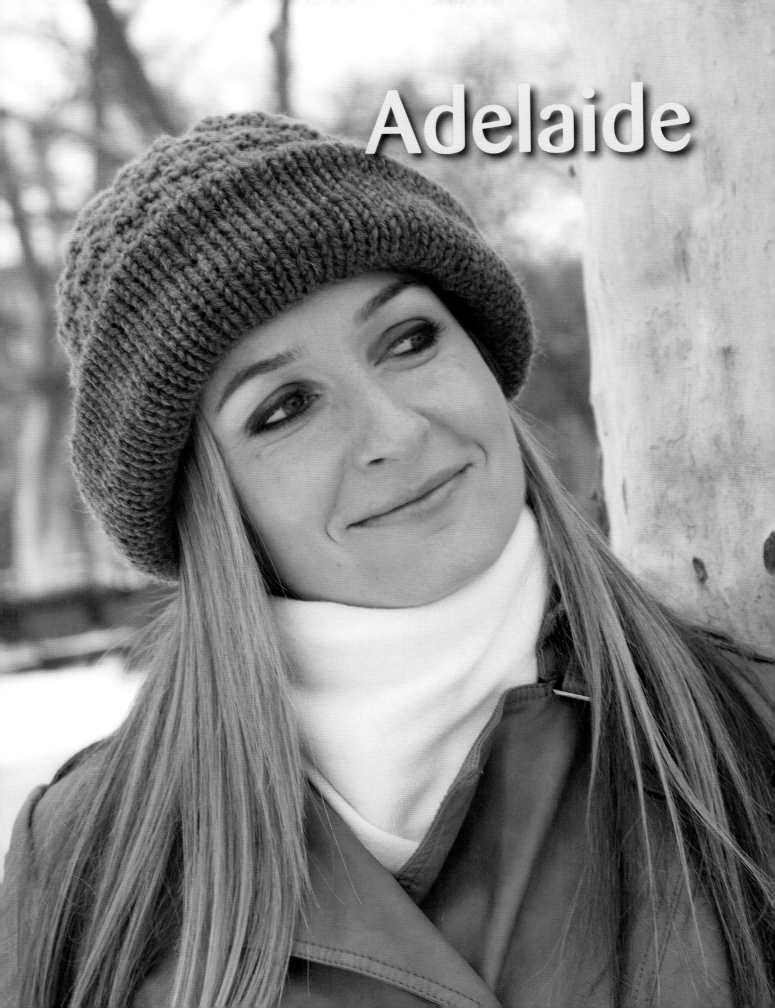
Adelaide

Adelaide Dunbar is a variety of French hybrid lilac bush. Known for its texture and tone-on-tone coloring, it was the perfect inspiration for this vintage-style cloche. The double-layered brim makes for a toasty and stylish winter hat.

FINISHED MEASUREMENTS

Circumference at brim band 22" (56 cm) unstretched, 10" (25 cm) in length from brim edge to crown, unfolded; will fit head circumference of 20" to 23" (50.5 to 58 cm)

YARN

Color A: 128 yds (117 m) super bulky #5 yarn (shown knitted in #1399 Smoky Violet, Cascade 128, 100% Peruvian Highland wool, 128 yds/117 m per skein)

Color B: 64 yds (56 m) super bulky #5 yarn (shown knitted in #2450 Purple, Cascade 128, 100% Peruvian Highland wool, 128 yds/117 m per skein)

NEEDLES AND OTHER MATERIALS

- One 16" (40.5 cm) circular knitting needle US 10 (6 mm) or size needed to obtain gauge
- US 10 (6 mm) set of 5 double-pointed needles or size needed to obtain gauge
- Stitch marker
- Scissors
- Yarn needle

GAUGE

14 sts x 18 rows in stitch pattern = 4" (10 cm) square

STITCH PATTERN

Rnds 1–2: *K1, p1; repeat from *around.
Rnds 3–4: *P1, k3; repeat from *around.
Rnds 5–6: *K1, p1; repeat from *around.
Rnds 7–8: K2, p1,*k3, p1; repeat from *around until last st, k1.

Note

- Hat is worked in rounds beginning with inside brim. Brim will fold inside hat at purl row; knit cast-on row and working sts together to hem.
- Switch from circular needles to double-pointed needles when necessary during crown shaping.

Cast On

Using long-tail method and circular needle, CO 64 sts with Color B. Place a stitch marker between first and last sts and join in the round, being careful not to twist the cast-on row.

Brim

Rnds 1–20: Knit.
Rnd 21: Purl.
Switch to Color A.
Rnds 22–25: Knit.
Rnds 26–41: Work entire stitch pattern 2 times.
Fold brim up at purl row to inside of hat. Matching row for row, pick up one stitch from the cast-on row and knit together with the working stitch of the same row, hemming the rows together. Work the entire hat brim hem around in this manner.

Body

Rnds 1–32: Work entire stitch pattern 4 times.

Crown Shaping

Rnd 1: *K1, p1, k1, p1, k1, p1, k2tog; rep from * around—56 sts.
Rnd 2: *K1, p1, k1, p1, k1, k2tog; rep from * around—48 sts.
Rnd 3: *P1, k3, k2tog; rep from * around—40 sts.
Rnd 4: *P1, k2, k2tog; rep from * around—32 sts.
Rnd 5: *K1, p1, k2tog; rep from * around—24 sts.
Rnd 6: *K1, k2tog; rep from * around—16 sts.
Rnd 7: *K2tog; rep from * around—8 sts.

Finishing

Cut yarn, leaving an 8" (20.5 cm) tail. Thread yarn needle with end and pick up remaining stitches on knitting needles. Pull tightly to close and secure end. Weave in yarn tails on inside of hat.

Turban

An alluring expression of glamour, the turban has been a Hollywood favorite for decades. This hat has a classic vintage feel that pairs well with both easygoing casual dress and your favorite designer outfits. Quick to knit, you'll want one in every color for every occasion. Worked up in a combination of stockinette and reverse stockinette, this is a great choice for beginners.

FINISHED MEASUREMENTS

Circumference at brim band 18" (46 cm) unstretched, 7" (18 cm) in length from brim edge to crown; will fit head circumference of 20" to 23" (50.5 to 58 cm)

YARN

120 yds (110 m) bulky weight #5 yarn (shown knitted in #1914 Emerald, Mirasol Kutama, 50% alpaca, 50% fine Highland wool, 67 yds/62 m per skein)

NEEDLES AND OTHER MATERIALS

· One 16" (40.5 cm) circular knitting needle US 8 (5 mm) or size needed to obtain gauge
· US 8 (5 mm) set of 5 double-pointed needles or size needed to obtain gauge
· Stitch marker
· Scissors
· Yarn needle

GAUGE

16 sts x 22 rows in stitch pattern = 4" (10 cm) square

Note

- Hat is worked in rounds from bottom edge to crown. Switch from circular needles to double-pointed needles when necessary during crown shaping.

Cast On

Using long-tail method and circular needle, CO 65 sts. Place a stitch marker between first and last sts and join in the round, being careful not to twist the cast-on row.

Body

Rnds 1–3: Purl.
Rnds 4–6: Knit.
Rnds 7–9: Purl.
Rnds 10–12: Knit.
Rnds 13–15: Purl.
Rnds 16–18: Knit.
Rnds 19–21: Purl.
Rnds 22–24: Knit.
Rnds 25–27: Purl.
Rnd 28: K32, then, with the working yarn, from back to front, tightly wrap the yarn around the knitted fabric from top to bottom 8 times to create the front "knot" of the hat, then knit the rem sts on the left needle.
Rnd 29: K31, k2tog, k32—64 sts.
Rnd 30: Knit.
Rnds 31–33: Purl.
Rnds 34–36: Knit.
Rnds 37–39: Purl.

Rnds 40–42: Knit.
Rnds 43–45: Purl.
Rnds 46–48: Knit.
Rnds 49–51: Purl.
Rnd 52: *K6, k2tog; rep from * around—56 sts.
Rnds 53–54: Knit.
Rnd 55: *P5, p2tog; rep from * around—48 sts.
Rnds 56–57: Purl.
Rnd 58: *K4, k2tog; rep from * around—40 sts.
Rnds 59–60: Knit.
Rnd 61: *P3, p2tog; rep from * around—32 sts.
Rnds 62–63: Purl.
Rnd 64: *K2, k2tog; rep from * around—24 sts.
Rnds 65–66: Knit.
Rnd 67: *K2tog; rep from * around—12 sts.

Finishing

Cut yarn, leaving an 8" (20.5 cm) tail. Thread yarn needle with end and pick up remaining stitches on knitting needles. Pull tightly to close and secure end. Weave in yarn tails on inside of hat.

Polar
Vortex

he whimsical spinning swirl of Polar Vortex can be worked with or without the button placket. To work without the placket, simply eliminate the beginning knitted stockinette stitches on your yarn-over repeat rows. Work those stitches as you would the rest of the repeated stitch pattern row. If worked with the placket, use the stockinette column to show off beautiful contrasting buttons.

FINISHED MEASUREMENTS
Circumference at brim band 17" (43 cm) unstretched, 8" (20 cm) in length from brim edge to crown; will fit head circumference of 20" to 23" (50.5 to 58 cm)

YARN
150 yds (137 m) bulky weight #5 yarn (shown knitted in #M10 Creme, Brown Sheep Company Lamb's Pride Bulky, 85% wool, 15% mohair, 125 yds/114 m per skein)

NEEDLES AND OTHER MATERIALS
- One 16" (40.5 cm) circular knitting needle US 10 (6 mm) or size needed to obtain gauge
- US 10 (6 mm) set of 5 double-pointed needles or size needed to obtain gauge
- Stitch marker
- Scissors
- Yarn needle
- Buttons (optional)

GAUGE
14 sts x 18 rows in stitch pattern = 4" (10 cm) square

STITCH PATTERN
Rnd 1: K8, *yo, sl1, k3, psso; rep from * around.
Rnd 2: Knit

Note

- Hat is worked in rounds from bottom edge to crown. Switch from circular needles to double-pointed needles when necessary during crown shaping.

Cast On

Using long-tail method and circular needle, CO 64 sts. Place stitch marker between first and last st and join in the round, being careful not to twist the cast-on row.

Brim

Rnds 1–10: *K2, p2; rep from * around.
Rnd 11: *K2, m1L; rep from * around—96 sts.

Body

Rnds 1–26: Work entire stitch pattern 13 times.

Crown Shaping

Rnd 1: K8, *yo, sl1, k3, psso; rep from * around.
Rnd 2: *K2, k2tog; rep from * around—72 sts.
Rnd 3: K6, *yo, sl1, k2, psso; rep from * around.
Rnd 4: *K1, k2tog; rep from * around—48 sts.
Rnd 5: K4, *yo, sl1, k1, psso; rep from * around.
Rnd 6: *K2tog; rep from * around—24 sts.
Rnd 7: *K2tog; rep from * around—12 sts.

Finishing

Cut yarn, leaving an 8" (20.5 cm) tail. Thread yarn needle with end and pick up remaining stitches on knitting needles. Pull tightly to close and secure end. Weave in yarn tails on inside of hat. Affix buttons to stockinette stitch strip down hat.

Gingham
Envelope

Gingham Envelope is a modern, casual knit with a recognizable checked color pattern. The unusual envelope shaping offers a refreshing change from a traditional decreased crown. The pattern provides both written instructions and a colorwork chart.

FINISHED MEASUREMENTS

Circumference at brim band 18" (46 cm) unstretched, 9.5" (24 cm) in length from brim edge to crown; will fit head circumference of 20" to 23" (50.5 to 58 cm)

YARN

Color A: 140 yds (128 m) worsted weight #4 yarn (shown knitted in #M151 Chocolate Souffle, Brown Sheep Company Lamb's Pride Worsted, 85% wool, 15% mohair, 190 yds/173 m per skein)

Color B: 110 yds (101 m) worsted weight #4 yarn (shown knitted in #M10 Crème, Brown Sheep Company Lamb's Pride Worsted, 85% wool, 15% mohair, 190 yds/173 m per skein)

NEEDLES AND OTHER MATERIALS

- One 16" (40.5 cm) circular knitting needle US 7 (4.5 mm) or size needed to obtain gauge
- One US 7 (4.5 mm) double-pointed needle or size needed to obtain gauge
- Stitch marker
- Scissors
- Yarn needle

GAUGE

20 sts x 26 rows in stockinette stitch = 4" (10 cm) square

GINGHAM PATTERN

Rnd 1: *K1B, k1A, k1B, k1A, k1B, k5A; rep from * around.

Rnd 2: *K1A, k1B, k1A, k1B, k6A; rep from * around.

Rnd 3: *K1B, k1A, k1B, k1A, k1B, k5A; rep from * around. (continued)

(continued from page 97)
Rnd 4: *K1A, k1B, k1A, k1B, k6A; rep from * around.
Rnd 5: *K1B, k1A, k1B, k1A, k1B, k5A; rep from * around.
Rnd 6: *K1A, k1B, k1A, k1B, k6A; rep from * around.
Rnd 7: *K5B, k1A, k1B, k1A, k1B, k1A; rep from * around.
Rnd 8: *K6B, k1A, k1B, k1A, k1B; rep from * around.
Rnd 9: *K5B, k1A, k1B, k1A, k1B, k1A; rep from * around.
Rnd 10: *K6B, k1A, k1B, k1A, k1B; rep from * around.
Rnd 11: *K5B, k1A, k1B, k1A, k1B, k1A; rep from * around.
Rnd 12: *K6B, k1A, k1B, k1A, k1B; rep from * around.

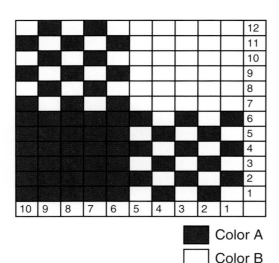

										12
										11
										10
										9
										8
										7
										6
										5
										4
										3
										2
										1
10	9	8	7	6	5	4	3	2	1	

■ Color A
□ Color B

Gingham Pattern

Note

- Hat is worked in rounds from bottom edge to top seam. The hat will be seamed from the inside with a three-needle bind-off; the corners will be folded in and sewn down.
- In the Gingham Pattern directions, A and B refer to the yarn colors.
- Color charts are read from bottom to top and from right to left.
- Knitting a pattern in two colors is called stranding. Only one color is knit at a time, while the other color will wait its turn and be carried behind the work until it is used again. Be certain that the carried yarn remains at a relaxed tension. When switching from one color to the other, Color A should always strand from underneath Color B and Color B should always be carried above Color A.
- For a photo tutorial on three-needle bind-off, see page 130.

Cast On

Using long-tail method and circular needle, CO 90 sts in Color A. Place a stitch marker between first and last sts and join in the round, being careful not to twist the cast-on row.

Brim

Rnds 1–8: *K1, p1; rep from * around.
Rnd 9: *K3, m1L; rep from * around—120 sts.

Body

Rnds 1–36: In stockinette stitch, work entire Gingham patt 3 times.

Finishing

Turn hat inside out. Cut Color A yarn, leaving an 8" (20.5 cm) tail. Using Color B and double-pointed needle, work a three-needle bind-off seam across top edge.

When you have one loop on your needle, cut the yarn, leaving an 8" (20.5 cm) tail; feed the tail through the remaining loop, and tighten.

Fold hat corners over about 1" (2.5 cm) each and sew to bind-off edge using tails. Weave in ends and turn hat right side out.

Tupelo
Beehive

A model of versatility, this hat can be worn with the ribbed brim folded or straight. This is a project where you can get away with a more ornate yarn, something with great texture or tweed details. Maybe take it up a notch by using a contrasting color for the knitted valleys of the body.

FINISHED MEASUREMENTS
Circumference at brim band 20" (51 cm) unstretched, 10" (25 cm) in length from brim edge to crown; will fit head circumference of 20" to 23" (50.5 to 58 cm)

YARN
150 yds (137 m) bulky weight #5 yarn (shown knitted in #292105, Debbie Bliss Donegal Chunky Tweed, 100% wool, 109 yds/100 m per skein)

NEEDLES AND OTHER MATERIALS
- One 16" (40.5 cm) circular knitting needle US 10.5 (6.5 mm) or size needed to obtain gauge
- US 10.5 (6.5 mm) set of 5 double-pointed needles or size needed to obtain gauge
- Stitch marker
- Scissors
- Yarn needle

GAUGE
14 sts x 18 rows in stockinette stitch = 4" (10 cm) square

Note

- Hat is worked in rounds from bottom edge to crown. Switch from circular needle to double-pointed needles when necessary during crown shaping.

Cast On

Using long-tail method and circular needle, CO 60 sts. Place a stitch marker between first and last sts and join in the round, being careful not to twist the cast-on row.

Brim

Rnds 1–24: *K2, p2; rep from * around.
Rnd 25: *K4, m1L; rep from * around—75 sts.

Body

Rnds 1–4: Purl.
Rnds 5–8: Knit.
Rnds 9–12: Purl.
Rnds 13–16: Knit.
Rnds 17–20: Purl.
Rnds 21–24: Knit.
Rnds 25–28: Purl.
Rnds 29–32: Knit.
Rnds 33–36: Purl.

Crown Shaping

Rnd 1: *K3, k2tog; rep from * around—60 sts.
Rnd 2: *K2, k2tog; rep from * around—45 sts.
Rnd 3: *K1, k2tog; rep from * around—30 sts.
Rnd 4: *K2tog; rep from * around—15 sts.

Finishing

Cut yarn, leaving an 8" (20.5 cm) tail. Thread yarn needle with end and pick up remaining stitches on knitting needles. Pull tightly to close and secure end. Weave in yarn tails on inside of hat.

How to Use This Book

A pattern is to a knitter what a recipe is to a chef. Our ingredients are skeins and balls and hanks of yarn; our weights and measures are gauge and yardage. Instead of mixers we use knitting needles. Instead of baking, we are blocking. We make test batches by knitting swatches, and we too use abbreviations for common and often-used words and phrases. This section will assist you in choosing the right materials and tools; aid you in deciphering charts, symbols, and abbreviations; and help you make the most of your knitting experience.

How to Read a Pattern

When deciding on a pattern, it is best to read all the instructions first, from beginning to end. Be sure it is suitable for your needs and offers the size you'll require or an explanation of how to alter it. Note the yarns and other supplies called for. Take into consideration the stitches and techniques employed in the pattern and your level of comfort with them. That being said, do not limit yourself. Acquiring a new skill is often just a short lesson away. Tutorials such as those offered in this book are incredibly useful (see pages 105–136), and there is also a bounty of information to be found on the Internet.

Some patterns in this book include charts and color grids. As all of these patterns are written to be knit in the round, the charts should be read from right to left, bottom to top, as you will always be working on the right side of the fabric. It is assumed that the pattern will be repeated to complete each round. Pattern stitch charts will include a chart key where each symbol represents a specific type of stitch.

Abbreviations

BO	bind off		pfb	purl into front and back of the stitch to increase
CC	contrasting color		psso	pass slipped stitch over
CO	cast on		RC	right cross (cable)
dpn(s)	double-pointed needle(s)		RCC	right cable crossover
k	knit		rep	repeat
k1tbl	knit one stitch through the back loop		rnd(s)	round(s)
k2tog	knit two stitches together		RPC	right purl cross (cable)
k5b	knit stitch 5 rows below		RS	right side of knitted fabric
kfb	knit into front and back of the stitch to increase		sl	slip
LC	left cross (cable)		sl1k	slip one stitch as if to knit
LPC	left purl cross (cable)		sl1p	slip one stitch as if to purl
m1L	left-leaning make one increase		smkst	smocking stitch
m1P	make one purl-wise		ssk	slip slip knit decrease
MC	main color		sts	stitches
p	purl		WS	wrong side of knitted fabric
p2tog	purl two stitches together		yo	yarn over
patt	pattern			

Sizing

Each pattern begins with an indication of what size head the finished garment should fit as well as the measurements of the finished piece lying flat and unstretched. Some patterns include instructions for more than one size. Most often I simply recommend going up or down a needle size to accommodate a different circumference.

Gauge

Gauge refers to the number of stitches and rows per inch in a particular pattern stitch while using a specific sized knitting needle and yarn. It is always best to knit your own swatch using this same combination of needle and yarn or a similar yarn substitution as referenced in the pattern. Use a tape measure or gauge tool to compare your stitch and row count to those suggested in the pattern. If the same gauge is not met, increase or decrease the size of the needle to counteract these differences.

Also be aware that you might not hit gauge spot on, as everyone knits with different tension, both across and vertically. What's most important for fit is that the number of stitches per inch matches gauge. If you've hit the stitch gauge but your gauge on rows is off—either more rows per inch or less rows per inch than what I'm calling for—you can fix that by adding or subtracting rows when knitting the body of the hat.

Needles and Tools

Knitting needles come in various sizes and materials as well as three types: straight, double-pointed, and circular. I most often design in the round using circular needles and therefore rarely use straight needles; even when knitting a flat piece, I tend to still knit on circulars, without joining. Each pattern will indicate the type and size needed, but the material they are made of is your choice.

Circular knitting is a way of knitting a tube that has no seams. When casting on your stitches, be careful not to twist the stitches on your foundation row before joining the stitches and always place a marker between the first and last stitches to mark the end of each round. As you're decreasing, switch to double-pointed needles before the knitting becomes too tight on the circular needle.

Other basic tools you will need include stitch markers, scissors, a yarn needle, a cable needle, and a ruler or gauge.

Yarn and Yarn Substitution

Let's get to everyone's favorite part—the yarn! My husband, who is also a knitter, is just as wide-eyed as I am when a new yarn magazine arrives in the mail. We'll circle our favorite colors, dog-ear the pages for quick reference, and practically mangle the poor magazine until it looks like a toy catalog three weeks before Christmas.

Patterns not only require a certain weight of yarn, but many patterns are only successful if the right texture and color are used as well. Dark yarns, for example, can mask cable details. Some yarns are highly textured, have a fuzzy halo, or have a strong variegated color pattern and are not appropriate for patterns with raised stitch detail. A smooth single-ply or multi-ply yarn that is not prone to splitting often works best for patterns that require sharp stitch definition. Often your designer has already done the legwork for you, choosing a type of yarn that is the right fit for the pattern.

If a yarn substitution is needed or desired, be certain to choose something that does not stray too far from the original. All of the information you will need is located on the yarn label. A checklist of things to be mindful of includes:

1. **Yarn weight:** The thickness of the yarn is referred to as yarn weight. There are six yarn weights—the higher the number, the heavier the yarn. Thinner yarns require smaller needles and will produce more stitches per inch; heavier yarns require larger needles and produce fewer stitches per inch. It is important to choose a yarn in the same weight class as intended in the pattern to produce a somewhat predictable amount of stitches per inch.

2. **Length per skein:** Length is typically measured in yards and/or meters. Be careful to purchase enough yarn for the entire project. Better to have a little too much than not enough. In every pattern I tell you the exact yardage the hat requires, so you don't end up getting caught short if you're substituting another yarn with a different skein length.

3. **Dye lot:** When purchasing multiple skeins of yarn, make certain they all come from the same dye lot, which will be stamped on the label. The same number means they were dyed in the same batch, ensuring that the color will be consistent from skein to skein. Skeins from different dye lots can vary in shade. An ombre look can be a nice design detail when intentional, but a real disaster when not.

4. **Fiber content:** Yarn is made from a wide range of materials, from wool to cotton to acrylic to blends of multiple fibers and more. Each fiber offers a different durability, ease of care, drape, and feel. When substituting a different yarn for the one originally intended, look for similarities in these characteristics. Novelty yarns are rarely a good choice for a knitted garment and should be reserved for accents.

5. **Needle suggestion and gauge:** You will notice a square yarn symbol on the label of each skein of yarn. It will include the suggested needle size (for both knitting and crochet) to use with this yarn and the amount of stitches and rows this combination should create when knit in stockinette pattern. Do not solely rely on this

information; you should still swatch your yarn as indicated in each of my patterns before beginning your project to ensure proper gauge.

6. Care instructions: Basic care instructions are usually included on the yarn ball band. They will let you know if this yarn should be exclusively hand washed or if it is machine washable, like a superwash wool. If it says to hand wash, please do, or you'll likely end up with a felted hat.

When it comes to quality and price, I always recommend purchasing the best quality yarn in your price range that meets the characteristics needed for the pattern. After all, if you are going to spend time creating the project, it would be a pity if your efforts were not long lasting or simply lost in translation because of a poor yarn choice. But far be it from me to engage in yarn snobbery. I have been known to knit with anything from bargain bin yarn to reclaimed thrift shop sweater yarn to yarn that was ridiculously outside my budget. Luxurious yarn, however tempting, is not always the best choice, and lesser priced yarns are not always the worst choice. That is to say, not all yarns are created equal, nor are all yarns suitable for every pattern, and price should only be one factor in the decision.

Blocking and Washing

Blocking your knits is a necessary step that many knitters overlook. Although more important for natural fibers than synthetics, blocking your knits helps to smooth out any inconsistencies in the stitches and bloom the yarn. When a project is finished, I suggest holding it over a steaming pot of water or misting it with a spray bottle. You may then either lay it flat to dry or position it over a balloon blown up to roughly your head size. Avoid overstretching ribbing.

To hand wash your knit, fill a basin with lukewarm water and add a mild detergent or yarn soak if desired. Avoid agitation and wringing; instead, you should pat and lightly press. Allow your knit to soak for a few minutes, then gently rinse the garment, supporting it so it does not stretch. Roll the garment in a towel, jelly-roll style, to pull out the remaining moisture. Lay the item flat to dry; do not allow it to hang.

Standard Yarn Weight System

Categories of yarn, gauge ranges, and recommended needle and hook sizes

Yarn Weight Symbol & Category Names	0 LACE	1 SUPER FINE	2 FINE	3 LIGHT	4 MEDIUM	5 BULKY	6 SUPER BULKY
Type of Yarns in Category	Fingering 10-count crochet thread	Sock, Fingering, Baby	Sport, Baby	DK, Light Worsted	Worsted, Afghan, Aran	Chunky, Craft, Rug	Bulky, Roving
Knit Gauge Range* in Stockinette Stitch to 4 inches	33–40** sts	27–32 sts	23–26 sts	21–24 st	16–20 sts	12–15 sts	6–11 sts
Recommended Needle in Metric Size Range	1.5–2.25 mm	2.25–3.25 mm	3.25–3.75 mm	3.75–4.5 mm	4.5–5.5 mm	5.5–8 mm	8 mm and larger
Recommended Needle U.S. Size Range	000–1	1 to 3	3 to 5	5 to 7	7 to 9	9 to 11	11 and larger
Crochet Gauge* Ranges in Single Crochet to 4 inches	32–42 double crochets**	21–32 sts	16–20 sts	12–17 sts	11–14 sts	8–11 sts	5–9 sts
Recommended Hook in Metric Size Range	Steel*** 1.6–1.4 mm	2.25–3.5 mm	3.5–4.5 mm	4.5–5.5 mm	5.5–6.5 mm	6.5–9 mm	9 mm and larger
Recommended Hook U.S. Size Range	Steel*** 6, 7, 8 Regular hook B-1	B-1 to E-4	E-4 to 7	7 to I-9	I-9 to K-10 ½	K-10 ½ to M-13	M-13 and larger

* GUIDELINES ONLY: The above reflect the most commonly used gauges and needle or hook sizes for specific yarn categories.

** Lace weight yarns are usually knitted or crocheted on larger needles and hooks to create lacy, openwork patterns. Accordingly, a gauge range is difficult to determine. Always follow the gauge stated in your pattern.

*** Steel crochet hooks are sized differently from regular hooks—the higher the number, the smaller the hook, which is the reverse of regular hook sizing.

This Standards & Guidelines booklet and downloadable symbol artwork are available at: YarnStandards.com

Stitches and Techniques

Whether you are learning something new or just need a refresher, tutorials can be useful for both experienced and novice knitters. The purpose of this section is to provide written and visual instructions for the knitting techniques used in this book. From casting on to binding off, following these simple step-by-step instructions should make even the most intimidating of patterns a piece of cake.

Casting On

All things that are built, like a bridge or a house or a relationship, need to start with a strong foundation, and knitting is no different. To begin a project, you must cast the yarn onto the knitting needle, creating a base row of stitches on which to build. There are dozens of different ways of casting on, but I will focus on three: the long-tail cast-on, the backward-loop cast-on, and the provisional crochet cast-on.

My go-to cast-on is the long-tail cast-on. I think it is the easiest to learn and creates a nice stable medium-stretch row that is easy to knit into.

Begin by estimating how much yarn is needed for the long tail. It should include roughly 1 inch of yarn per cast-on stitch plus 6 to 8 inches for weaving in when the garment is finished.

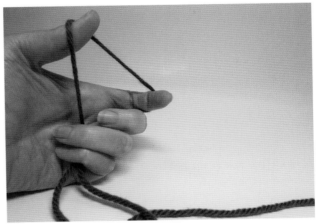

1. Position your hand as though it is holding an invisible slingshot. Drape the yarn over your hand with the long tail end over the thumb and the working yarn over the index finger. Gather these two strands in your palm with your other three fingers. Do not hold this yarn too tightly; as you build the row, these strands will need to flow with an even tension. (continued)

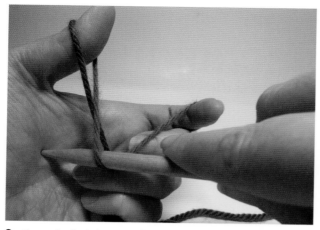

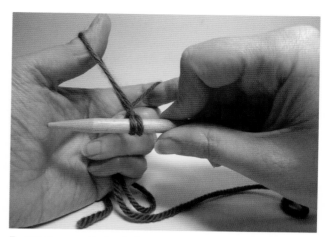

2. Press the knitting needle down onto the length of yarn that is between the thumb and index finger to form a V.

5. Tilt the needle back down into the loop around the thumb.

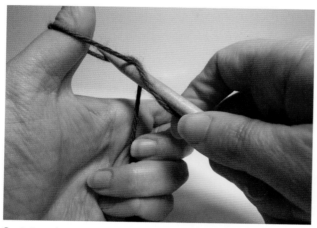

3. Bring the needle up into the loop that has been formed around the thumb.

6. Let go of the yarn around the thumb and pull down on the tail end to snug the loop to the needle. Avoid tightening the stitch too much. Following these steps the first time will result in two stitches on the needle.

4. Turn your wrist so that your thumb is now pointing at you and use the needle to scoop up the length of yarn that is strung between the index finger and palm.

7. Repeat steps 3–6 for each additional stitch.

Backward Loop Cast-On

I reserve this particular cast-on for when I am casting on stitches between knitted sections within a project, such as between ear flaps. A backward loop cast-on is not as stretchy as a long-tail cast-on and can be tricky to knit into.

1. Using the working yarn, create a loop of yarn around your thumb.

2. Place this loop backwards on the needle.

3. Tighten down this loop by tugging slightly on the working yarn.

4. Repeat these steps for each additional stitch.

Provisional Crochet Cast-On

A provisional crochet cast-on is worked over a scrap piece of yarn that will later be removed to expose live stitches. These live stitches can then be worked from seamlessly. This is helpful when a project requires that a beginning edge and finished edge should be invisibly seamed together.

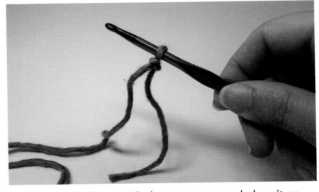

1. Create a slip knot with the scrap yarn and place it on the crochet hook.

2. Hold the knitting needle in your left hand and the crochet hook in your right hand, with the working end of the scrap yarn behind the needle. (continued)

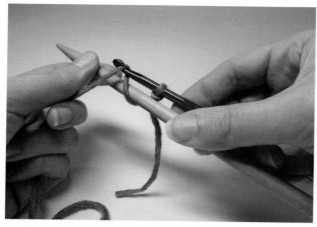

3. Hook the scrap yarn with your crochet hook, covering the knitting needle.

4. Draw the yarn through the loop on the hook, encasing the knitting needle in a loop of yarn.

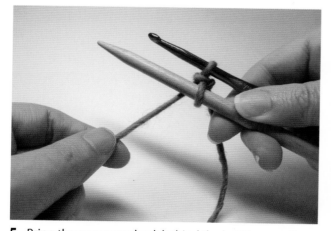

5. Bring the scrap yarn back behind the knitting needle.

6. Repeat these steps for each additional stitch.

7. Crochet chain four additional stitches after the cast-on row so you can readily identify which end to unravel later.

8. Cut tail and secure the loose end.

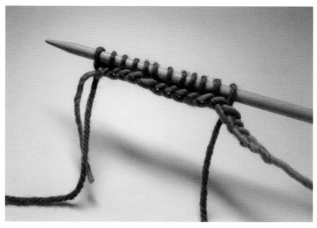

9. Switch to the working yarn and knit across the crochet stitches. Continue the project as written.

10. To remove the provisional cast on, begin by untying the knot in the scrap yarn at the end with the four additional crochet stitches.

11. Unravel the extra stitches.

12. Unravel the first stitch, exposing the live stitch.

13. Insert a knitting needle into the live stitch, where the scrap yarn was.

14. Continue down the row, exposing each live stitch and inserting the needle into it until the row is completely on the needle and free of the scrap yarn.

Basic Stitches

Knitted fabric is made up of interlocking building blocks that create length, width, and texture. Patterns will call for different configurations of these blocks to create the finished piece. Learning the basics is essential, as well as a couple of variations on these techniques.

Knit (k)

1. Holding the working yarn behind the needles, insert the right needle into the front of the first stitch on the left needle from left to right.

2. Wrap the yarn around the right needle counterclockwise.

3. Pull the yarn through the stitch.

4. Slip the stitch off the left needle.

Purl (p)

1. Holding the working yarn in front of your needles, insert the right needle into the front of the first stitch on the left needle from right to left.

2. Wrap the yarn around the right needle counterclockwise.

3. Pull the yarn through the stitch.

4. Slip the stitch off the left needle.

Yarn Over (yo)

Wrap the yarn around the right needle counterclockwise.

Slip (sl) a Stitch

1. Insert the right needle into the first stitch on the left needle as if to knit.

2. Slide the stitch off the left needle onto the right needle.

Knit 1 Through the Back Loop (k1tbl)

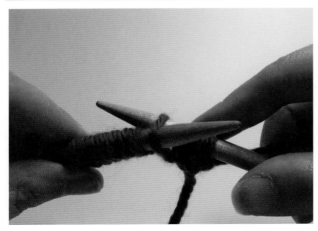

1. Holding the working yarn behind the needles, insert the right needle into the back of the first stitch on the left needle from right to left.

2. Wrap the yarn around the right needle counterclockwise.

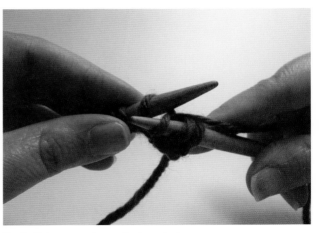

3. Pull the yarn through the stitch.

4. Slip the stitch off the left needle.

Cables and Texture Stitches

Put simply, knitted cables are achieved by knitting stitches out of order, crossing layers of knitted fabric over one another. Textures are accomplished by manipulating basic stitches, sometimes in a slightly unusual way. Both techniques can turn a very basic project into something extraordinary.

Left Purl Cross (LPC)

1. Slip 1 stitch to a cable needle.

2. Hold the cable needle to the front of the work.

3. Purl 1 stitch from the main needle.

4. Knit 1 stitch from the cable needle.

Left Purl Cross

Right Purl Cross (RPC)

1. Slip 1 stitch to a cable needle.

2. Hold the cable needle to the back of the work.

3. Knit 1 stitch from the main needle.

4. Purl 1 stitch from the cable needle.

Right Purl Cross

2/2 Left Cross (2/2 LC)

1. Slip next 2 stitches to a cable needle.

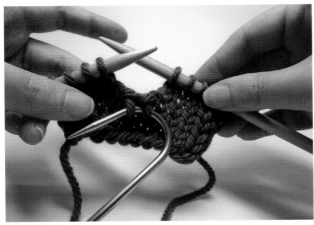

2. Hold the cable needle to the front of the work.

2/2 Left Cross

3. Knit 2 stitches from the main needle.

2/2 Right Cross (2/2 RC)

1. Slip next 2 stitches to a cable needle.

4. Knit 2 stitches from the cable needle.

2. Hold the cable needle to the back of the work.
(continued)

3. Knit 2 stitches from the main needle.

4. Knit 2 stitches from the cable needle.

2/2 Right Cross

2/2 Left Purl Cross (2/2 LPC)

1. Slip next 2 stitches to a cable needle.

2. Hold the cable needle to the front of the work.

3. Purl 2 stitches from the main needle.

4. Knit 2 stitches from the cable needle.

2/2 Left Purl Cross

2/2 Right Purl Cross (2/2 RPC)

1. Slip next 2 stitches to a cable needle.

2. Hold the cable needle to the back of the work.

3. Knit 2 stitches from the main needle.

4. Purl 2 stitches from the cable needle. (continued)

2/2 Right Purl Cross

3. Knit 3 stitches from the main needle.

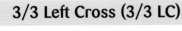
3/3 Left Cross (3/3 LC)

1. Slip next 3 stitches to a cable needle.

4. Knit 3 stitches from the cable needle.

3/3 Left Cross

2. Hold the cable needle to the front of the work.

3/3 Right Cross (3/3 RC)

1. Slip next 3 stitches to a cable needle.

2. Hold the cable needle to the back of the work.

3. Knit 3 stitches from the main needle.

4. Knit 3 stitches from the cable needle.

3/3 Right Cross

6 Stitch Right Cable Crossover (6RCC)

1. Slip next 3 stitches to a cable needle.

2. Hold the cable needle to the back of the work.

3. Knit next 2 stitches from the main needle.

4. Replace purl stitch from the cable needle back onto the left hand needle and purl.

5. Knit 2 stitches from the cable needle.

6. Purl next stitch.

6 Stitch Right Cable Crossover

3. Knit stitch, gathering the 4 strands behind the stitch with it.

Knit Stitch 5 Rows Below (k5b)

1. Slip next stitch off the left needle and carefully let it drop 4 rows.

2. Insert right needle into front of dropped stitch and under the 4 loose strands.

Smocking Stitch (smkst)

1. Insert the right needle between stitches 6 and 7 on the left needle.

2. Wrap the right needle with the working yarn counterclockwise.

3. Pull a loop of working yarn through and place it on the end of the left needle.

4. Knit this new loop together with the first stitch.

I-cord

1. Using long-tail method and 2 double-pointed needles, cast on 4 stitches.

2. Knit across.

3. Slide the work to the right end of the dpn. Do not turn the work.

4. With the working yarn coming around the back from the left-most stitch, knit into the right-most stitch and continue knitting the row.

5. Repeat steps 3 and 4 until desired length.

Shaping

Increasing and decreasing the number of stitches in a row will allow you to alter the shape of knitting. Typically, in this book, I will use increases to add more volume to a hat and decreases to slope a crown.

Make 1 Left Increase (m1L)

This make 1 increase creates a smooth new left-leaning knit stitch between two other stitches. This is an easy general increase that adds width without leaving a large hole or loop.

1. Insert the left needle from front to back into the horizontal strand between the stitches on the right and left needles.

2. Knit the lifted loop through the back.

Make 1 Purl Increase (m1P)

The make 1 purl increase creates an identical purl stitch between two existing purl stitches.

1. Insert the left needle from back to front into the horizontal strand between the stitches on the right and left needles.

2. Purl the lifted loop through the front.

Knit Front and Back Increase (kfb)

This increase will leave you with a decorative bar at the base of the second stitch.

1. Knit into the next stitch, leaving it on the left needle.

2. Bring the tip of the right needle around to the back of the stitch and knit into the back loop of the same stitch.

3. Slip the stitches off the left needle.

Purl Front and Back Increase (pfb)

1. Purl into the next stitch, leaving it on the left needle.

2. Bring the tip of the right needle around to the back of the stitch and purl into the back loop of the same stitch.

3. Slip the stitches off the left needle.

Knit 2 Together Decrease (k2tog)

This is probably the most commonly used decrease. It creates a decrease that slants to the right.

1. Insert the right needle into the first two stitches on the left needle.

2. Knit these stitches together as though they are one stitch.

Purl 2 Together Decrease (p2tog)

1. Insert the right needle into the first two stitches on the left needle.

2. Purl these stitches together as though they are one stitch.

Slip, Slip, Knit Decrease (ssk)

This decrease slants to the left.

1. Use the tip of your right needle to slip the first stitch off the left needle knitwise.

2. Use the tip of your right needle to slip the second stitch off the left needle knitwise.

3. Insert the left needle into these 2 stitches on the right needle.

4. Knit these stitches together as though they are one stitch.

Slip 1, Knit 1, Pass Slipped Stitch Over Decrease (sl1, k1, psso)

1. Use the tip of your right needle to slip the first stitch off the left needle knitwise.

2. Knit the next stitch.

3. Pass the slipped stitch on the right needle over the knitted stitch and off the needle.

Finishing

You're in the home stretch! Securing your new project from unraveling is of utmost importance. First, you must get it off the needles. Binding off your knitting is a process of ending each column of stitches and providing a finished edge or gather. This section will also cover how to join two live rows for a nearly invisible seam.

Cinching Up a Hat

Truly the easiest technique possible for securing the crown of a hat.

1. Cut the yarn, leaving an 8" (20.5 cm) tail.

2. Thread a yarn needle with the end and pick up the remaining stitches on the knitting needle(s).

3. Pull tightly to close and secure the end.

4. Weave in the yarn tail on the inside of the hat.

Bind Off (BO)

When simply instructed to BO, this is the method to use:

1. Knit 2 stitches.

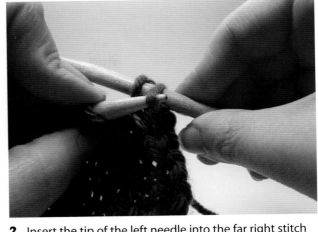

2. Insert the tip of the left needle into the far right stitch on the right needle.

3. Lift the stitch up and over the left stitch on the right needle and off the needle.

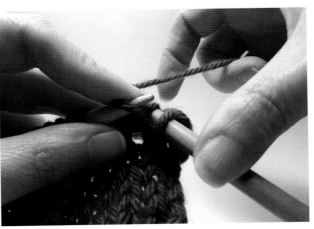

4. Knit the next stitch on the left needle. (continued)

5. Repeat steps 2–4 until all stitches are bound. Cut the yarn leaving an 8" (20.5 cm) tail and secure it through the remaining loop on the right needle.

Three-Needle Bind-Off

For this, you will bind off across two needles of live stitches to create a neat seam.

1. Hold both points of your circular needle to the right.

2. Using a third needle, knit together one stitch from the front needle and one stitch from the back needle as though they were one stitch.

3. Repeat this action, using the new first loops on the front and back needles.

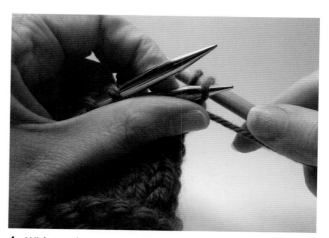

4. With two loops now on your third needle, insert the tip of the left needle into the far right stitch on the third needle.

5. Lift the stitch up and over the left stitch on the third needle and off the needle.

6. Repeat steps 3 through 5 until all stitches are bound. Cut the yarn, leaving an 8" (20.5 cm) tail, and secure it through the remaining loop on the right needle.

Kitchener Stitch

Kitchener stitch is a way of grafting two live rows of knitting together from the outside of the work to form an almost invisible seam.

1. First you will need to do an anchor row. Hold your needles parallel, pointing toward the right. Cut your working yarn, leaving a tail one and a half times the length of the seam. Thread a yarn needle and insert it into the first stitch of the front needle as if to purl and draw the yarn through, leaving the stitch on the knitting needle.

2. Now insert the yarn needle into the first stitch on the back knitting needle as if to knit; draw the yarn through, leaving the stitch on the knitting needle. (continued)

3. Now we will begin the process of grafting. Insert the yarn needle into the first stitch of the front knitting needle as if to knit and draw the yarn through. Slip this stitch off the knitting needle.

6. Insert the yarn needle into the second stitch of the back knitting needle as if to knit and draw the yarn through. Leave this stitch on the knitting needle.

7. Repeat steps 3–6 to continue grafting the live stitches together, occasionally tugging your tail yarn to tighten.

4. Insert the yarn needle into the second stitch of the front knitting needle as if to purl and draw the yarn through. Leave this stitch on the knitting needle.

The seam is visible on the wrong side of the fabric

5. Insert the yarn needle into the first stitch of the back knitting needle as if to purl and draw the yarn through. Slip this stitch off the knitting needle.

The seam is invisible on the right side

Embellishments

Embellishments can add a great deal of character and personality to a piece. Pom-poms and tassels serve a double purpose in that they can also add weight to hold down otherwise floppy strips of knitted fabric and twisted cords for drawstrings and ties. They're an ideal way of using up the leftover bits of yarn from your project.

Pom-Poms

1. To make a 2" (5 cm) pom-pom, hold the three middle fingers of your hand together and wrap yarn around them until the desired thickness.

2. Cut the yarn end and cut another piece of yarn about 8" (20.5 cm) in length.

3. Slide the bundle of yarn off your fingers, tightly pinching the middle of the bundle. Wrap the 8" (20.5 cm) piece of yarn around the middle of the bundle three times and double knot tightly.

4. Cut through the two end bundles of loops to free the pom-pom pieces.

5. Shape and trim as needed, being careful not to cut the tails of the center knot yarn.
   Attach the pom-pom by tying its long tails into the knitting. Trim ends.

Tassels

1. To make a 6" (15 cm) tassel, cut a 6" (15 cm) long piece of cardboard.

2. Cut two pieces of yarn 13" (33 cm) each and set aside.

3. Wrap the working yarn around the cardboard 30 or more times, depending on how thick you would like the tassel to be, and cut the end of yarn on the same side where the wrapping began.

4. Slide one of the 13" (33 cm) pieces of yarn under the opposite end and double knot tightly.

5. Slide scissors between the cardboard and the yarn at the opposite end and cut the yarn to free the tassel.

6. Hold the tassel firmly and wrap the second 13" (33 cm) piece of yarn around the bundle twice about 1" (2.5 cm) from the top knot and double knot tightly.

When attaching to the project, feed the top knot tails through the tip of the hat and secure, then use the yarn needle to feed those ends down through the tassel. Trim ends as needed.

Twisted Cord

1. Cut two pieces of yarn four times as long as the desired finished length. Held together, fold yarn in half, and secure the looped end around a door knob or tape to a table.

2. Tie a knot at the open end to secure and slip a pen or pencil through this loop.

3. Pull the yarn taut and twist the pencil clockwise. Continue twisting until the yarn doubles back on itself when slack is given. (continued)

4. Bring the ends together and smooth out the cord to make it even.

5. Tie an overhand knot leaving a 1" (2.5 cm) section at each end.

6. Cut the ends to free the fringe.

Visual Index

Rural Pathways 2

Sophisti-Cat 5

Portsmouth Watchman 9

Trapper 12

Steps & Ladders 15

Sidewinder 18

Cozy Cable 21

Greenwich 24

Slalom 27

Spanish Moss 30

Mariner 33

Helmet 36

Fairway 39

Mulligan 42

Coaxial 46

Bubble Gum 49

 Urchin 52

 Grape Jellyfish 55

 Kaleidoscope 58

 Smocking Stocking Cap 62

 Ribs & Twists 66

 Vermont Foliage 69

 Native American Geometric 73

 Jubilee 77

 Twofer 80

 Rhubarb 84

 Adelaide 87

 Turban 90

 Polar Vortex 93

 Gingham Envelope 96

 Tupelo Beehive 99